Thanks for choosing The Ultimate RV Logbook!
You're holding an amazing tool for your travel adventures. We,
wanted to produce something that would actually be useful for

M000007439

Our goal was to create a place where you can record all of the great (and sometimes not
so great) notes & impressions of your camping spots as you wander about in your RV. We
made this book a place to store information but also easily find those notes again later, so
we incorporated an easy-to-use referencing system, organized by U.S. state (or you can fill in
your own regions). This way, when you need to look back on your notes from two, three, or
even 20 years later, you will be able to quickly find them.

Here's how to use this book:

1. **Log Your Stays:** Turn to the first log and start writing! Use our prompted checkoffs to
record basic info and then also add your own notes as a refresher for your memory later. We
didn't make a checkbox for every possible scenario (there are so many!)
So, use the extra space to write down anything you think you might want to know later.
For instance, you may note more things like low/high water pressure, road noise, or
management/staff names & notes. Did you spend way too much on laundry here? Make a
note of it! Did you see a sasquatch walk casually through your campground on Friday night?
Make a note of it! And share the picture! You did get one, right?

2. **Our Referencing System:** It's so simple! Let's begin with the Site Logs. Each Site Log has
a number in the corner. When you log a campsite, take a second to record that site's Log
Number in the back of the book in its reference section. Most reference sections are simply
a state. However, some states are larger (and more popular) than others, so we broke them
down into smaller regions for even quicker reference. For instance, we've broken Texas down
to 5 regions: North, West, Central, Gulf Coast & Panhandle.

3. **Maintenance Logs:** In the back of the book, there are pages dedicated for recording RV
maintenance. Just record the date, service performed, mileage, and any other notes there so
you have that information later. ·

4. **Filled up the book?** When this one is filled, simply reorder! Or, get a new one each year
so you can clearly keep your travels organized by year for reference later. Just search The
Ultimate RV Logbook on Amazon and choose yours. There are multiple cover designs to
choose from! Be sure to select the one by "Nomadic Souls Gear & Apparel".

We hope you love this logbook!
Brandon & Brit Cave
Nomadic Souls Gear & Apparel

Check out our other editions and cover options as well as our Ultimate Hiking Logbook and Ultimate Campfire Guest Book!

Just search Amazon for your favorite edition's ISBN to order a different design.

Classic Original Cover
ISBN: 978-1790403660

Fulltime Families Edition
Exclusive Family Content!
ISBN:978-1792891847

Leather-look Cover
ISBN: 978-1790808342

Vintage Travel Poster Edition
ISBN: 9798679660632

Ultimate Hiking Logbook
ISBN: 978-1702409865

Campfire Guest Book
ISBN: 979-8656183178

Nomadic Souls
GEAR & APPAREL
WWW.NOMADICSOULSGEAR.COM

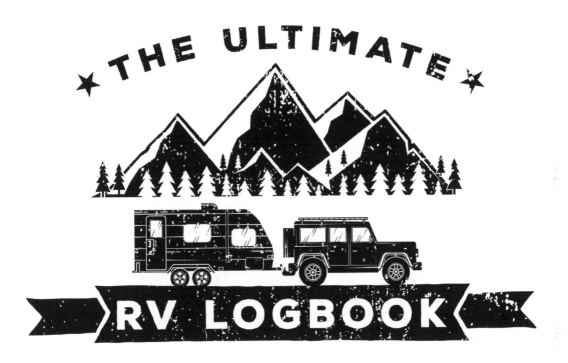

THE ULTIMATE
RV LOGBOOK

THE MOST EFFICIENT WAY TO
RECORD AND REFERENCE YOUR
CAMPSITES AS YOU TRAVEL.

WWW.NOMADICSOULSGEAR.COM

NATIONAL PARKS:

JR RANGER BADGES:

- ⬩ Acadia National Park, ME • Date:
- ⬩ Arches National Park, UT • Date:
- ⬩ Badlands National Park, SD • Date:
- ⬩ Big Bend National Park, TX • Date:
- ⬩ Biscayne National Park, FL • Date:
- ⬩ Black Canyon of the Gunnison, CO • Date:
- ⬩ Bryce Canyon National Park, UT • Date:
- ⬩ Canyonlands National Park, UT • Date:
- ⬩ Capitol Reef National Park, UT • Date:
- ⬩ Carlsbad Caverns National Park, NM • Date:
- ⬩ Channel Islands National Park, CA • Date:
- ⬩ Congaree National Park, South CA • Date:
- ⬩ Crater Lake National Park, OR • Date:
- ⬩ Cuyahoga Valley National Park, OH • Date:
- ⬩ Death Valley National Park, CA & NV • Date:
- ⬩ Denali National Park, AK • Date:
- ⬩ Dry Tortugas National Park, FL • Date:
- ⬩ Everglades National Park, FL • Date:
- ⬩ Gates of the Arctic NP & Preserve, AK • Date:
- ⬩ Glacier National Park, MT • Date:
- ⬩ Glacier Bay NP and Preserve, AK • Date:
- ⬩ Grand Canyon National Park, AZ • Date:
- ⬩ Grand Teton National Park, WY • Date:
- ⬩ Great Basin National Park, NV • Date:
- ⬩ Great Sand Dunes NP & Preserve, CO • Date:
- ⬩ Great Smoky Mountains NP, NC & TN • Date:
- ⬩ Guadalupe Mountains NP, TX • Date:
- ⬩ Haleakalā National Park, HI • Date:
- ⬩ Hawaii Volcanoes NP, HI • Date:
- ⬩ Hot Springs National Park, AR • Date:

NATIONAL PARKS: JR RANGER BADGES:

◇ Isle Royale National Park, MI • Date:

◇ Joshua Tree National Park, CA • Date:

◇ Katmai NP and Preserve, AK • Date:

◇ Kenai Fjords National Park, AK • Date:

◇ Kings Canyon National Park, CA • Date:

◇ Kobuk Valley National Park, AK • Date:

◇ Lake Clark NP & Preserve, AK • Date:

◇ Lassen Volcanic National Park, CA • Date:

◇ Mammoth Cave National Park, KY • Date:

◇ Mesa Verde National Park, CO • Date:

◇ Mount Rainier National Park, WA • Date:

◇ NP of American Samoa, American Samoa • Date:

◇ North Cascades National Park, WA • Date:

◇ Olympic National Park, WA • Date:

◇ Petrified Forest National Park, AZ • Date:

◇ Pinnacles National Park, CA • Date:

◇ Redwood National Park, CA • Date:

◇ Rocky Mountain National Park, CO • Date:

◇ Saguaro National Park, AZ • Date:

◇ Sequoia National Park, CA • Date:

◇ Shenandoah National Park, VA • Date:

◇ Theodore Roosevelt NP, ND • Date:

◇ Virgin Islands NP, US Virgin Islands • Date:

◇ Voyageurs National Park, MN • Date:

◇ Wind Cave National Park, SD • Date:

◇ Wrangell-StElias NP & Preserve, AK • Date:

◇ Yellowstone NP, WY, ID, and MT • Date:

◇ Yosemite National Park, CA • Date:

◇ Zion National Park, UT • Date:

Campground: _____ **Date(s):** ___ / ___ / ___

Location/Address/GPS: _____

Travel to Campground Miles: _____ Time: _____ Travel notes: _____

Cost(s): _____

General Campground/Park Notes:

Hookups: FHU: ○Some ○All ○W/E Only ○50&30 Amp ○30 Amp Only ○Dry Camping
○Dump Station Other hookups notes:_____

Bathhouse: ○ Flush Toilets ○Showers (○FREE ○Quarters) Enough Hot Water? ○Y ○N

Cleanliness: 1 2 3 4 5 (1= very dirty, 5= squeaky clean)

Other bathhouse notes: _____

Amenities: ○Pool ○Hot Tub ○Lodge/Game Room ○Adult Ctr ○Laundry ○Restaurant
○Shuffleboard ○Pickleball ○Mini Golf ○Pet-Friendly ○ Dog Park
○Hiking ○Canoeing ○Fishing ○Horseback Riding ○Fitness Center

Other amenity notes:_____
_____

Management/Booking/Cancellation Notes: _____
_____

Any Campground Scenery? _____
_____

Maneuvering/Parking: ○Tight roads/turns ○Low-hanging trees ○Bad road conditions
Other parking notes:_____
_____
_____

Site-specific Notes: Site Number Stayed In: [_____]

Site Hookups: ○FHU ○W/E Only ○50 Amp ○30 Amp ○Dry Camping

RV Pad: ○Level ○Unlevel ○Concrete ○Rock ○Grass ○Dirt ○Other: _____

Site size: ○Tight ○Moderate ○Spacious ○Very large

Trees/Shade: ○Full Sun ○Some shade ○A lot of shade

Fire ring/pit? ○Y○N Fires allowed?○Y○N Picnic table?○Y○N Nice view? ○Y ○N

Close to Amenities? ○Very Close ○Easy Walk ○Too far to walk

Noise: ○Quiet ○Light Road Noise ○Loud Road Noise ○Train ○Other:_____

Any wildlife, bugs, etc? _____

Other site-specific notes: _____

Local Area Notes:

Weather During Stay: ○Very Cold ○Cold ○Moderate ○Warm ○Hot

Other weather notes: _____

Nearby Sightseeing: _____

_____

Nearby Restaurants: _____

_____

Nearest Grocery Store: ○0-5 mi ○5-10 mi ○10-20mi ○20-30mi ○30+ mi

Other grocery or provisions notes: _____

Nearby places visited: _____

_____

_____

_____

Visit/do next time: _____

_____

_____

Connectivity Notes: Wi-Fi: ○Y ○N Rating: 1 2 3 4 5 (1= horrible, 5= excellent)

Cellular signal: Verizon ▯▯▮▮ AT&T ▯▯▮▮ Sprint ▯▯▮ T-Mobile ▯▯▮ _____ ▯▮▮

Other Notes: _____

_____

Other notes: _____

_____

_____

_____

_____

_____

_____

_____

_____

_____

_____

Campground: _____ **Date(s):** _____ / _____ / _____

Location/Address/GPS: _____

Travel to Campground Miles: _____ Time: _____ Travel notes: _____

Cost(s): _____

General Campground/Park Notes:

Hookups: FHU: ○Some ○All ○W/E Only ○50&30 Amp ○30 Amp Only ○Dry Camping
○Dump Station   Other hookups notes:_____

Bathhouse: ○ Flush Toilets ○Showers (○FREE ○Quarters)   Enough Hot Water? ○Y ○N
Cleanliness: 1 2 3 4 5 (1= very dirty, 5= squeaky clean)
Other bathhouse notes: _____

Amenities: ○Pool ○Hot Tub ○Lodge/Game Room ○Adult Ctr ○Laundry ○Restaurant
○Shuffleboard ○Pickleball ○Mini Golf ○Pet-Friendly ○ Dog Park
○Hiking ○Canoeing ○Fishing ○Horseback Riding ○Fitness Center

Other amenity notes:_____
_____

Management/Booking/Cancellation Notes: _____
_____

Any Campground Scenery?_____
_____

Maneuvering/Parking: ○Tight roads/turns ○Low-hanging trees ○Bad road conditions
Other parking notes:_____
_____
_____

Site-specific Notes: Site Number Stayed In: [   ]

Site Hookups: ○FHU ○W/E Only ○50 Amp ○30 Amp ○Dry Camping

RV Pad: ○Level○Unlevel ○Concrete ○Rock ○Grass ○Dirt ○Other: _____

Site size: ○Tight ○Moderate ○Spacious ○Very large

Trees/Shade: ○Full Sun ○Some shade ○A lot of shade

Fire ring/pit? ○Y○N   Fires allowed?○Y○N   Picnic table?○Y○N   Nice view? ○Y○N

Close to Amenities? ○Very Close ○Easy Walk ○Too far to walk

Noise: ○Quiet ○Light Road Noise ○Loud Road Noise ○Train ○Other:_____

Any wildlife, bugs, etc? _____

Other site-specific notes: _____

Local Area Notes:

Weather During Stay: ○Very Cold ○Cold ○Moderate ○Warm ○Hot

Other weather notes: _____

Nearby Sightseeing: _____

_____

Nearby Restaurants: _____

_____

Nearest Grocery Store: ○0-5 mi ○5-10 mi ○10-20mi ○20-30mi ○30+ mi

Other grocery or provisions notes: _____

Nearby places visited: _____

_____

_____

Visit/do next time: _____

_____

_____

Connectivity Notes: Wi-Fi: ○Y ○N Rating: 1 2 3 4 5 (1= horrible, 5= excellent)

Cellular signal: Verizon ▫▫▫ AT&T ▫▫▫ Sprint ▫▫▫ T-Mobile ▫▫▫ _____ ▫▫▫

Other Notes: _____

_____

Other notes: _____

_____

_____

_____

_____

_____

_____

_____

_____

_____

Don't forget to add this Log Number to your reference section in the back!

Campground: _____ **Date(s):** ____ / ____ / ____

Location/Address/GPS: _____

Travel to Campground Miles: _____ Time: _____ Travel notes: _____

Cost(s): _____

General Campground/Park Notes:

Hookups: FHU: ○Some ○All ○W/E Only   ○50&30 Amp ○30 Amp Only ○Dry Camping
○Dump Station Other hookups notes:_____

Bathhouse: ○Flush Toilets ○Showers (○FREE ○Quarters) Enough Hot Water? ○Y ○N
Cleanliness: 1 2 3 4 5 (1= very dirty, 5= squeaky clean)
Other bathhouse notes: _____

Amenities: ○Pool ○Hot Tub ○Lodge/Game Room ○Adult Ctr ○Laundry ○Restaurant
○Shuffleboard ○Pickleball ○Mini Golf ○Pet-Friendly ○Dog Park
○Hiking ○Canoeing ○Fishing ○Horseback Riding ○Fitness Center

Other amenity notes:_____
_____

Management/Booking/Cancellation Notes: _____
_____

Any Campground Scenery?_____
_____

Maneuvering/Parking: ○Tight roads/turns ○Low-hanging trees   ○Bad road conditions
Other parking notes:_____
_____
_____

Site-specific Notes: Site Number Stayed In: [_____]

Site Hookups: ○FHU   ○W/E Only   ○50 Amp   ○30 Amp   ○Dry Camping

RV Pad: ○Level○Unlevel   ○Concrete ○Rock ○Grass ○Dirt ○Other: _____

Site size: ○Tight ○Moderate ○Spacious ○Very large

Trees/Shade: ○Full Sun ○Some shade ○A lot of shade

Fire ring/pit? ○Y○N   Fires allowed?○Y○N   Picnic table?○Y○N Nice view? ○Y ○N

Close to Amenities? ○Very Close ○Easy Walk ○Too far to walk

Noise: ○Quiet ○Light Road Noise ○Loud Road Noise ○Train ○Other:_____

Any wildlife, bugs, etc? _____

Other site-specific notes: _____

Local Area Notes:

Weather During Stay: ○Very Cold ○Cold ○Moderate ○Warm ○Hot

Other weather notes: _____

Nearby Sightseeing: _____

_____

Nearby Restaurants: _____

_____

Nearest Grocery Store: ○ 0-5 mi ○ 5-10 mi ○ 10-20mi ○ 20-30mi ○ 30+ mi

Other grocery or provisions notes: _____

Nearby places visited: _____

_____

_____

_____

Visit/do next time: _____

_____

_____

Connectivity Notes: Wi-Fi: ○Y ○N   Rating: 1 2 3 4 5 (1= horrible, 5= excellent)

Cellular signal: Verizon ▫▫▫▫ AT&T ▫▫▫▫ Sprint ▫▫▫▫ T-Mobile ▫▫▫▫ _____ ▫▫▫▫

Other Notes: _____

_____

Other notes: _____

_____

_____

_____

_____

_____

_____

_____

_____

_____

_____

Campground: _____ **Date(s):** ____ / ____ / ____

Location/Address/GPS: _____

Travel to Campground Miles: _____ Time: _____ Travel notes: _____

Cost(s): _____

General Campground/Park Notes:

Hookups: FHU: ○Some ○All ○W/E Only ○50&30 Amp ○30 Amp Only ○Dry Camping
○Dump Station Other hookups notes:_____

Bathhouse: ○ Flush Toilets ○Showers (○FREE ○Quarters) Enough Hot Water? ○Y ○N

Cleanliness: 1 2 3 4 5 (1= very dirty, 5= squeaky clean)

Other bathhouse notes: _____

Amenities: ○Pool ○Hot Tub ○Lodge/Game Room ○Adult Ctr ○Laundry ○Restaurant
○Shuffleboard ○Pickleball ○Mini Golf ○Pet-Friendly ○ Dog Park
○Hiking ○Canoeing ○Fishing ○Horseback Riding ○Fitness Center

Other amenity notes:_____
_____

Management/Booking/Cancellation Notes: _____
_____

Any Campground Scenery? _____
_____

Maneuvering/Parking: ○Tight roads/turns ○Low-hanging trees ○Bad road conditions

Other parking notes:_____
_____
_____

Site-specific Notes: Site Number Stayed In: [_____]

Site Hookups: ○FHU ○W/E Only ○50 Amp ○30 Amp ○ Dry Camping

RV Pad: ○Level○Unlevel ○Concrete ○Rock ○Grass ○Dirt ○Other: _____

Site size: ○Tight ○Moderate ○Spacious ○Very large

Trees/Shade: ○Full Sun ○ Some shade ○A lot of shade

Fire ring/pit? ○Y○N Fires allowed?○Y ○N Picnic table?○Y ○N Nice view? ○Y ○N

Close to Amenities? ○Very Close ○Easy Walk ○Too far to walk

Noise: ○Quiet ○Light Road Noise ○Loud Road Noise ○Train ○Other:_____

Any wildlife, bugs, etc? _____

Other site-specific notes: _____

Local Area Notes:

Weather During Stay: ○Very Cold ○Cold ○Moderate ○Warm ○Hot

Other weather notes: _____

Nearby Sightseeing: _____

_____

Nearby Restaurants: _____

_____

Nearest Grocery Store: ○0-5 mi ○5-10 mi ○10-20mi ○20-30mi ○30+ mi

Other grocery or provisions notes:_____

Nearby places visited:_____

_____

_____

Visit/do next time:_____

_____

_____

Connectivity Notes: Wi-Fi: ○Y ○N Rating: 1 2 3 4 5 (1= horrible, 5= excellent)

Cellular signal: Verizon ▢▢▢ AT&T ▢▢▢ Sprint ▢▢▢ T-Mobile ▢▢▢ _____ ▢▢▢

Other Notes: _____

_____

Other notes:_____

_____

_____

_____

_____

_____

_____

_____

_____

_____

_____

Campground: _____ **Date(s):** ___ / ___ / ___

Location/Address/GPS: _____

Travel to Campground Miles: _____ Time: _____ Travel notes: _____

Cost(s): _____

General Campground/Park Notes:

Hookups: FHU: ○Some ○All ○W/E Only ○50&30 Amp ○30 Amp Only ○Dry Camping
○Dump Station   Other hookups notes:_____

Bathhouse: ○Flush Toilets ○Showers (○FREE ○Quarters)   Enough Hot Water? ○Y ○N
Cleanliness: 1 2 3 4 5 (1= very dirty, 5= squeaky clean)
Other bathhouse notes: _____

Amenities: ○Pool ○Hot Tub ○Lodge/Game Room ○Adult Ctr ○Laundry ○Restaurant
○Shuffleboard ○Pickleball ○Mini Golf ○Pet-Friendly ○Dog Park
○Hiking ○Canoeing ○Fishing ○Horseback Riding ○Fitness Center

Other amenity notes:_____
_____

Management/Booking/Cancellation Notes: _____
_____

Any Campground Scenery?_____
_____

Maneuvering/Parking: ○Tight roads/turns ○Low-hanging trees ○Bad road conditions
Other parking notes:_____
_____
_____

Site-specific Notes: Site Number Stayed In: [_____]

Site Hookups: ○FHU ○W/E Only ○50 Amp ○30 Amp ○Dry Camping

RV Pad: ○Level ○Unlevel ○Concrete ○Rock ○Grass ○Dirt ○Other: _____

Site size: ○Tight ○Moderate ○Spacious ○Very large

Trees/Shade: ○Full Sun ○Some shade ○A lot of shade

Fire ring/pit? ○Y ○N   Fires allowed? ○Y ○N   Picnic table? ○Y ○N   Nice view? ○Y ○N

Close to Amenities? ○Very Close ○Easy Walk ○Too far to walk

Noise: ○Quiet ○Light Road Noise ○Loud Road Noise ○Train ○Other:_____

Any wildlife, bugs, etc? _____

Other site-specific notes: _____

Local Area Notes:

Weather During Stay: ○Very Cold ○Cold ○Moderate ○Warm ○Hot

Other weather notes: _____

Nearby Sightseeing: _____

_____

Nearby Restaurants: _____

_____

Nearest Grocery Store: ○0-5 mi ○5-10 mi ○10-20mi ○20-30mi ○30+ mi

Other grocery or provisions notes:_____

Nearby places visited:_____

_____

_____

_____

Visit/do next time:_____

_____

_____

Connectivity Notes: Wi-Fi: ○Y ○N Rating: 1 2 3 4 5 (1= horrible, 5= excellent)

Cellular signal: Verizon ▫▫▫ AT&T ▫▫▫ Sprint ▫▫▫ T-Mobile ▫▫▫ _____ ▫▫▫

Other Notes: _____

_____

Other notes:_____

_____

_____

_____

_____

_____

_____

_____

_____

_____

_____

_____

Don't forget to add this Log Number to your reference section in the back!

Campground: _____ **Date(s):** ___ / ___ / ___

Location/Address/GPS: _____

Travel to Campground Miles: _____ Time: _____ Travel notes: _____

Cost(s): _____

General Campground/Park Notes:

Hookups: FHU: ○Some ○All ○W/E Only   ○50&30 Amp ○30 Amp Only ○Dry Camping
○Dump Station   Other hookups notes:_____

Bathhouse: ○ Flush Toilets   ○Showers (○FREE ○Quarters) Enough Hot Water? ○Y ○N
Cleanliness: 1 2 3 4 5 (1= very dirty, 5= squeaky clean)
Other bathhouse notes: _____

Amenities: ○Pool ○Hot Tub ○Lodge/Game Room ○Adult Ctr ○Laundry ○Restaurant
○Shuffleboard ○Pickleball ○Mini Golf ○Pet-Friendly ○ Dog Park
○Hiking ○Canoeing ○Fishing ○Horseback Riding ○Fitness Center

Other amenity notes:_____
_____

Management/Booking/Cancellation Notes: _____
_____

Any Campground Scenery?_____
_____

Maneuvering/Parking: ○Tight roads/turns ○Low-hanging trees ○Bad road conditions
Other parking notes:_____
_____
_____

Site-specific Notes: Site Number Stayed In: [_____]

Site Hookups: ○FHU   ○W/E Only   ○50 Amp   ○30 Amp   ○Dry Camping

RV Pad: ○Level ○Unlevel   ○Concrete ○Rock ○Grass ○Dirt ○Other: _____

Site size: ○Tight ○Moderate ○Spacious ○Very large

Trees/Shade: ○Full Sun ○Some shade ○A lot of shade

Fire ring/pit? ○Y ○N   Fires allowed? ○Y ○N   Picnic table? ○Y ○N   Nice view? ○Y ○N

Close to Amenities? ○Very Close ○Easy Walk ○Too far to walk

Noise: ○Quiet ○Light Road Noise ○Loud Road Noise ○Train ○Other:_____

Any wildlife, bugs, etc? _____

Other site-specific notes: _____

Local Area Notes:

Weather During Stay: ◯Very Cold ◯Cold ◯Moderate ◯Warm ◯Hot

Other weather notes: _____

Nearby Sightseeing: _____

_____

Nearby Restaurants: _____

_____

Nearest Grocery Store: ◯0-5 mi ◯5-10 mi ◯10-20mi ◯20-30mi ◯30+ mi

Other grocery or provisions notes: _____

Nearby places visited: _____

_____

_____

Visit/do next time: _____

_____

_____

Connectivity Notes: Wi-Fi: ◯Y ◯N   Rating: 1 2 3 4 5 (1= horrible, 5= excellent)

Cellular signal: Verizon ▫▫▫▫ AT&T ▫▫▫▫ Sprint ▫▫▫▫ T-Mobile ▫▫▫▫ _____ ▫▫▫▫

Other Notes: _____

_____

Other notes: _____

_____

_____

_____

_____

_____

_____

_____

_____

_____

_____

Don't forget to add this Log Number to your reference section in the back!

Campground: _____ **Date(s):** ___ / ___ / ___

Location/Address/GPS: _____

Travel to Campground Miles: _____ Time: _____ Travel notes: _____

Cost(s): _____

General Campground/Park Notes:

Hookups: FHU: ○Some ○All ○W/E Only ○50&30 Amp ○30 Amp Only ○Dry Camping
　　　　　○Dump Station　Other hookups notes:_____

Bathhouse: ○Flush Toilets ○Showers (○FREE ○Quarters)　Enough Hot Water? ○Y ○N
　　　　　Cleanliness: 1 2 3 4 5 (1= very dirty, 5= squeaky clean)
　　　　　Other bathhouse notes: _____

Amenities: ○Pool ○Hot Tub ○Lodge/Game Room ○Adult Ctr ○Laundry ○Restaurant
　　　　　○Shuffleboard ○Pickleball ○Mini Golf ○Pet-Friendly ○Dog Park
　　　　　○Hiking ○Canoeing ○Fishing ○Horseback Riding ○Fitness Center

Other amenity notes:_____
_____

Management/Booking/Cancellation Notes: _____
_____

Any Campground Scenery?_____
_____

Maneuvering/Parking: ○Tight roads/turns ○Low-hanging trees ○Bad road conditions
Other parking notes:_____
_____
_____

Site-specific Notes:　　　　Site Number Stayed In: [_____]

Site Hookups: ○FHU ○W/E Only ○50 Amp ○30 Amp ○Dry Camping

RV Pad: ○Level ○Unlevel ○Concrete ○Rock ○Grass ○Dirt ○Other: _____

Site size: ○Tight ○Moderate ○Spacious ○Very large

Trees/Shade: ○Full Sun ○Some shade ○A lot of shade

Fire ring/pit? ○Y ○N　Fires allowed? ○Y ○N　Picnic table? ○Y ○N　Nice view? ○Y ○N

Close to Amenities? ○Very Close ○Easy Walk ○Too far to walk

Noise: ○Quiet ○Light Road Noise ○Loud Road Noise ○Train ○Other:_____

Any wildlife, bugs, etc? _____

Other site-specific notes: _____

Local Area Notes:

Weather During Stay: ◯Very Cold ◯Cold ◯Moderate ◯Warm ◯Hot

Other weather notes: _____

Nearby Sightseeing: _____

_____

Nearby Restaurants: _____

_____

Nearest Grocery Store: ◯0-5 mi ◯5-10 mi ◯10-20mi ◯20-30mi ◯30+ mi

Other grocery or provisions notes: _____

Nearby places visited: _____

_____

_____

Visit/do next time: _____

_____

_____

Connectivity Notes: Wi-Fi: ◯Y ◯N Rating: 1 2 3 4 5 (1= horrible, 5= excellent)

Cellular signal: Verizon ▁▃▅ AT&T ▁▃▅ Sprint ▁▃▅ T-Mobile ▁▃▅ _____ ▁▃▅

Other Notes: _____

_____

Other notes: _____

_____

_____

_____

_____

_____

_____

_____

_____

_____

_____

Don't forget to add this Log Number to your reference section in the back!

Campground: _____ **Date(s):** ____ / ____ / ____

Location/Address/GPS: _____

Travel to Campground Miles: _____ Time: _____ Travel notes: _____

Cost(s): _____

General Campground/Park Notes:

Hookups: FHU: ◯Some ◯All ◯W/E Only ◯50&30 Amp ◯30 Amp Only ◯Dry Camping
◯Dump Station   Other hookups notes:_____

Bathhouse: ◯Flush Toilets ◯Showers (◯FREE ◯Quarters) Enough Hot Water? ◯Y ◯N
Cleanliness: 1 2 3 4 5 (1= very dirty, 5= squeaky clean)
Other bathhouse notes: _____

Amenities: ◯Pool ◯Hot Tub ◯Lodge/Game Room ◯Adult Ctr ◯Laundry ◯Restaurant
◯Shuffleboard ◯Pickleball ◯Mini Golf ◯Pet-Friendly ◯Dog Park
◯Hiking ◯Canoeing ◯Fishing ◯Horseback Riding ◯Fitness Center

Other amenity notes:_____
_____

Management/Booking/Cancellation Notes: _____
_____

Any Campground Scenery?_____
_____

Maneuvering/Parking: ◯Tight roads/turns ◯Low-hanging trees ◯Bad road conditions
Other parking notes:_____
_____
_____

Site-specific Notes: Site Number Stayed In: [   ]

Site Hookups: ◯FHU ◯W/E Only ◯50 Amp ◯30 Amp ◯Dry Camping
RV Pad: ◯Level◯Unlevel ◯Concrete ◯Rock ◯Grass ◯Dirt ◯Other: _____
Site size: ◯Tight ◯Moderate ◯Spacious ◯Very large
Trees/Shade: ◯Full Sun ◯Some shade ◯A lot of shade
Fire ring/pit? ◯Y◯N   Fires allowed?◯Y◯N   Picnic table?◯Y◯N   Nice view? ◯Y◯N
Close to Amenities? ◯Very Close ◯Easy Walk ◯Too far to walk
Noise: ◯Quiet ◯Light Road Noise ◯Loud Road Noise ◯Train ◯Other:_____
Any wildlife, bugs, etc? _____
Other site-specific notes:_____

Local Area Notes:

Weather During Stay: ○Very Cold ○Cold ○Moderate ○Warm ○Hot

Other weather notes: _____

Nearby Sightseeing: _____

_____

Nearby Restaurants: _____

_____

Nearest Grocery Store: ○0-5 mi ○5-10 mi ○10-20mi ○20-30mi ○30+ mi

Other grocery or provisions notes: _____

Nearby places visited: _____

_____

_____

Visit/do next time: _____

_____

_____

Connectivity Notes: Wi-Fi: ○Y ○N Rating: 1 2 3 4 5 (1= horrible, 5= excellent)

Cellular signal: Verizon ▭ AT&T ▭ Sprint ▭ T-Mobile ▭ _____ ▭

Other Notes: _____

_____

Other notes: _____

_____

_____

_____

_____

_____

_____

_____

_____

_____

_____

LOG NUMBER

8

Campground: _____ **Date(s):** ___ / ___ / ___

Location/Address/GPS: _____

Travel to Campground Miles: _____ Time: _____ Travel notes: _____
Cost(s): _____

General Campground/Park Notes:

Hookups: FHU: ○Some ○All ○W/E Only ○50&30 Amp ○30 Amp Only ○Dry Camping
○Dump Station   Other hookups notes:_____

Bathhouse: ○Flush Toilets ○Showers (○FREE ○Quarters) Enough Hot Water? ○Y ○N
Cleanliness: 1 2 3 4 5 (1= very dirty, 5= squeaky clean)
Other bathhouse notes: _____

Amenities: ○Pool ○Hot Tub ○Lodge/Game Room ○Adult Ctr ○Laundry ○Restaurant
○Shuffleboard ○Pickleball ○Mini Golf ○Pet-Friendly ○Dog Park
○Hiking ○Canoeing ○Fishing ○Horseback Riding ○Fitness Center

Other amenity notes:_____
_____

Management/Booking/Cancellation Notes: _____
_____

Any Campground Scenery?_____
_____

Maneuvering/Parking: ○Tight roads/turns ○Low-hanging trees ○Bad road conditions
Other parking notes:_____
_____
_____

Site-specific Notes: Site Number Stayed In: [_____]

Site Hookups: ○FHU ○W/E Only ○50 Amp ○30 Amp ○Dry Camping
RV Pad: ○Level ○Unlevel ○Concrete ○Rock ○Grass ○Dirt ○Other: _____
Site size: ○Tight ○Moderate ○Spacious ○Very large
Trees/Shade: ○Full Sun ○Some shade ○A lot of shade
Fire ring/pit? ○Y ○N Fires allowed? ○Y ○N Picnic table? ○Y ○N Nice view? ○Y ○N
Close to Amenities? ○Very Close ○Easy Walk ○Too far to walk
Noise: ○Quiet ○Light Road Noise ○Loud Road Noise ○Train ○Other:_____
Any wildlife, bugs, etc? _____
Other site-specific notes: _____

Local Area Notes:

Weather During Stay: ◯Very Cold ◯Cold ◯Moderate ◯Warm ◯Hot

Other weather notes: _____

Nearby Sightseeing: _____

_____

Nearby Restaurants: _____

_____

Nearest Grocery Store: ◯0-5 mi ◯5-10 mi ◯10-20mi ◯20-30mi ◯30+ mi

Other grocery or provisions notes: _____

Nearby places visited: _____

_____

_____

_____

Visit/do next time: _____

_____

_____

Connectivity Notes: Wi-Fi: ◯Y ◯N   Rating: 1 2 3 4 5 (1= horrible, 5= excellent)

Cellular signal: Verizon ▯▯▯ AT&T ▯▯▯ Sprint ▯▯▯ T-Mobile ▯▯▯ _____ ▯▯▯

Other Notes: _____

_____

Other notes: _____

_____

_____

_____

_____

_____

_____

_____

_____

_____

_____

_____

Campground: _____ **Date(s):** ___ / ___ / ___

Location/Address/GPS: _____

Travel to Campground Miles: _____ Time: _____ Travel notes: _____

Cost(s): _____

General Campground/Park Notes:

Hookups: FHU: ○Some ○All ○W/E Only ○50&30 Amp ○30 Amp Only ○Dry Camping
○Dump Station   Other hookups notes:_____

Bathhouse: ○Flush Toilets ○Showers (○FREE ○Quarters) Enough Hot Water? ○Y ○N
Cleanliness: 1 2 3 4 5 (1= very dirty, 5= squeaky clean)
Other bathhouse notes: _____

Amenities: ○Pool ○Hot Tub ○Lodge/Game Room ○Adult Ctr ○Laundry ○Restaurant
○Shuffleboard ○Pickleball ○Mini Golf ○Pet-Friendly ○Dog Park
○Hiking ○Canoeing ○Fishing ○Horseback Riding ○Fitness Center

Other amenity notes:_____
_____

Management/Booking/Cancellation Notes: _____
_____

Any Campground Scenery?_____
_____

Maneuvering/Parking: ○Tight roads/turns ○Low-hanging trees ○Bad road conditions
Other parking notes:_____
_____
_____

Site-specific Notes: Site Number Stayed In:[_____]

Site Hookups: ○FHU ○W/E Only ○50 Amp ○30 Amp ○Dry Camping

RV Pad: ○Level ○Unlevel ○Concrete ○Rock ○Grass ○Dirt ○Other: _____

Site size: ○Tight ○Moderate ○Spacious ○Very large

Trees/Shade: ○Full Sun ○Some shade ○A lot of shade

Fire ring/pit? ○Y ○N   Fires allowed? ○Y ○N   Picnic table? ○Y ○N   Nice view? ○Y ○N

Close to Amenities? ○Very Close ○Easy Walk ○Too far to walk

Noise: ○Quiet ○Light Road Noise ○Loud Road Noise ○Train ○Other:_____

Any wildlife, bugs, etc? _____

Other site-specific notes: _____

Local Area Notes:

Weather During Stay: ○Very Cold ○Cold ○Moderate ○Warm ○Hot

Other weather notes: _____

Nearby Sightseeing: _____

_____

Nearby Restaurants: _____

_____

Nearest Grocery Store: ○0-5 mi ○5-10 mi ○10-20mi ○20-30mi ○30+ mi

Other grocery or provisions notes: _____

Nearby places visited: _____

_____

_____

_____

Visit/do next time: _____

_____

_____

Connectivity Notes: Wi-Fi: ○Y ○N Rating: 1 2 3 4 5 (1= horrible, 5= excellent)

Cellular signal: Verizon ▫▫▫ AT&T ▫▫▫ Sprint ▫▫▫ T-Mobile ▫▫▫ _____ ▫▫▫

Other Notes: _____

_____

Other notes: _____

_____

_____

_____

_____

_____

_____

_____

_____

_____

_____

_____

_____

Campground: _____ **Date(s):** ___ / ___ / ___

Location/Address/GPS: _____

Travel to Campground Miles: _____ Time: _____ Travel notes: _____

Cost(s): _____

General Campground/Park Notes:

Hookups: FHU: ○Some ○All ○W/E Only ○50&30 Amp ○30 Amp Only ○Dry Camping
○Dump Station   Other hookups notes:_____

Bathhouse: ○Flush Toilets ○Showers (○FREE ○Quarters) Enough Hot Water? ○Y ○N
Cleanliness: 1 2 3 4 5 (1= very dirty, 5= squeaky clean)
Other bathhouse notes: _____

Amenities: ○Pool ○Hot Tub ○Lodge/Game Room ○Adult Ctr ○Laundry ○Restaurant
○Shuffleboard ○Pickleball ○Mini Golf ○Pet-Friendly ○Dog Park
○Hiking ○Canoeing ○Fishing ○Horseback Riding ○Fitness Center

Other amenity notes:_____
_____

Management/Booking/Cancellation Notes: _____
_____

Any Campground Scenery?_____
_____

Maneuvering/Parking: ○Tight roads/turns ○Low-hanging trees ○Bad road conditions
Other parking notes:_____
_____
_____

Site-specific Notes: Site Number Stayed In: [_____]

Site Hookups: ○FHU ○W/E Only ○50 Amp ○30 Amp ○Dry Camping

RV Pad: ○Level○Unlevel ○Concrete ○Rock ○Grass ○Dirt ○Other: _____

Site size: ○Tight ○Moderate ○Spacious ○Very large

Trees/Shade: ○Full Sun ○Some shade ○A lot of shade

Fire ring/pit? ○Y○N Fires allowed?○Y○N Picnic table?○Y○N Nice view? ○Y ○N

Close to Amenities? ○Very Close ○Easy Walk ○Too far to walk

Noise: ○Quiet ○Light Road Noise ○Loud Road Noise ○Train ○Other:_____

Any wildlife, bugs, etc? _____

Other site-specific notes: _____

Local Area Notes:

Weather During Stay: ◯Very Cold ◯Cold ◯Moderate ◯Warm ◯Hot

Other weather notes:_____

Nearby Sightseeing:_____

_____

Nearby Restaurants:_____

_____

Nearest Grocery Store: ◯0-5 mi ◯5-10 mi ◯10-20mi ◯20-30mi ◯30+ mi

Other grocery or provisions notes:_____

Nearby places visited:_____

_____

_____

_____

Visit/do next time:_____

_____

_____

Connectivity Notes: Wi-Fi: ◯Y ◯N Rating: 1 2 3 4 5 (1= horrible, 5= excellent)

Cellular signal: Verizon ▯▯▯ AT&T ▯▯▯ Sprint ▯▯▯ T-Mobile ▯▯▯ _____ ▯▯▯

Other Notes: _____

_____

Other notes:_____

_____

_____

_____

_____

_____

_____

_____

_____

_____

_____

_____

Don't forget to add this Log Number to your reference section in the back!

Campground: _____ **Date(s):** ____ / ____ / ____

Location/Address/GPS: _____

Travel to Campground Miles: _____ Time: _____ Travel notes: _____

Cost(s): _____

General Campground/Park Notes:

Hookups: FHU: ○Some ○All ○W/E Only ○50&30 Amp ○30 Amp Only ○Dry Camping
○Dump Station Other hookups notes:_____

Bathhouse: ○Flush Toilets ○Showers (○FREE ○Quarters) Enough Hot Water? ○Y ○N
Cleanliness: 1 2 3 4 5 (1= very dirty, 5= squeaky clean)
Other bathhouse notes: _____

Amenities: ○Pool ○Hot Tub ○Lodge/Game Room ○Adult Ctr ○Laundry ○Restaurant
○Shuffleboard ○Pickleball ○Mini Golf ○Pet-Friendly ○Dog Park
○Hiking ○Canoeing ○Fishing ○Horseback Riding ○Fitness Center

Other amenity notes:_____
_____

Management/Booking/Cancellation Notes: _____
_____

Any Campground Scenery?_____
_____

Maneuvering/Parking: ○Tight roads/turns ○Low-hanging trees ○Bad road conditions
Other parking notes:_____
_____
_____

Site-specific Notes: Site Number Stayed In:[_____]

Site Hookups: ○FHU ○W/E Only ○50 Amp ○30 Amp ○Dry Camping

RV Pad: ○Level ○Unlevel ○Concrete ○Rock ○Grass ○Dirt ○Other: _____

Site size: ○Tight ○Moderate ○Spacious ○Very large

Trees/Shade: ○Full Sun ○Some shade ○A lot of shade

Fire ring/pit? ○Y ○N Fires allowed? ○Y ○N Picnic table? ○Y ○N Nice view? ○Y ○N

Close to Amenities? ○Very Close ○Easy Walk ○Too far to walk

Noise: ○Quiet ○Light Road Noise ○Loud Road Noise ○Train ○Other:_____

Any wildlife, bugs, etc? _____

Other site-specific notes:_____

Local Area Notes:

Weather During Stay: ○Very Cold ○Cold ○Moderate ○Warm ○Hot

Other weather notes: _____

Nearby Sightseeing: _____

_____

Nearby Restaurants: _____

_____

Nearest Grocery Store: ○0-5 mi ○5-10 mi ○10-20mi ○20-30mi ○30+ mi

Other grocery or provisions notes:_____

Nearby places visited:_____

_____

_____

_____

Visit/do next time:_____

_____

_____

Connectivity Notes: Wi-Fi: ○Y ○N Rating: 1 2 3 4 5 (1= horrible, 5= excellent)

Cellular signal: Verizon ▫▫▫ AT&T ▫▫▫ Sprint ▫▫▫ T-Mobile ▫▫▫ _____ ▫▫▫

Other Notes: _____

_____

Other notes:_____

_____

_____

_____

_____

_____

_____

_____

_____

_____

_____

_____

Campground: _____ **Date(s):** ___ / ___ / ___

Location/Address/GPS: _____

Travel to Campground Miles: _____ Time: _____ Travel notes: _____

Cost(s): _____

General Campground/Park Notes:

Hookups: FHU: ○Some ○All ○W/E Only ○50&30 Amp ○30 Amp Only ○Dry Camping

○Dump Station   Other hookups notes:_____

Bathhouse: ○Flush Toilets ○Showers (○FREE ○Quarters) Enough Hot Water? ○Y ○N

Cleanliness: 1 2 3 4 5 (1= very dirty, 5= squeaky clean)

Other bathhouse notes: _____

Amenities: ○Pool ○Hot Tub ○Lodge/Game Room ○Adult Ctr ○Laundry ○Restaurant

○Shuffleboard ○Pickleball ○Mini Golf ○Pet-Friendly ○Dog Park

○Hiking ○Canoeing ○Fishing ○Horseback Riding ○Fitness Center

Other amenity notes:_____

_____

Management/Booking/Cancellation Notes: _____

_____

Any Campground Scenery?_____

_____

Maneuvering/Parking: ○Tight roads/turns ○Low-hanging trees ○Bad road conditions

Other parking notes:_____

_____

_____

Site-specific Notes: Site Number Stayed In: [_____]

Site Hookups: ○FHU ○W/E Only ○50 Amp ○30 Amp ○Dry Camping

RV Pad: ○Level ○Unlevel ○Concrete ○Rock ○Grass ○Dirt ○Other: _____

Site size: ○Tight ○Moderate ○Spacious ○Very large

Trees/Shade: ○Full Sun ○Some shade ○A lot of shade

Fire ring/pit? ○Y ○N   Fires allowed? ○Y ○N   Picnic table? ○Y ○N   Nice view? ○Y ○N

Close to Amenities? ○Very Close ○Easy Walk ○Too far to walk

Noise: ○Quiet ○Light Road Noise ○Loud Road Noise ○Train ○Other:_____

Any wildlife, bugs, etc? _____

Other site-specific notes: _____

Local Area Notes:

Weather During Stay: ○Very Cold ○Cold ○Moderate ○Warm ○Hot

Other weather notes: _____

Nearby Sightseeing: _____

_____

Nearby Restaurants: _____

_____

Nearest Grocery Store: ○0-5 mi ○5-10 mi ○10-20mi ○ 20-30mi ○ 30+ mi

Other grocery or provisions notes: _____

Nearby places visited: _____

_____

_____

_____

Visit/do next time: _____

_____

_____

Connectivity Notes: Wi-Fi: ○Y ○N   Rating: 1 2 3 4 5 (1= horrible, 5= excellent)

Cellular signal: Verizon ▫▫▫▫ AT&T ▫▫▫▫ Sprint ▫▫▫▫ T-Mobile ▫▫▫▫ _____ ▫▫▫▫

Other Notes: _____

_____

Other notes: _____

_____

_____

_____

_____

_____

_____

_____

_____

_____

_____

Don't forget to add this Log Number to your reference section in the back!

Campground: _____ **Date(s):** _____ / _____ / _____

Location/Address/GPS: _____

Travel to Campground Miles: _____ Time: _____ Travel notes: _____
Cost(s): _____

General Campground/Park Notes:

Hookups: FHU: ○Some ○All ○W/E Only ○50&30 Amp ○30 Amp Only ○Dry Camping
○Dump Station Other hookups notes:_____

Bathhouse: ○Flush Toilets ○Showers (○FREE ○Quarters) Enough Hot Water? ○Y ○N
Cleanliness: 1 2 3 4 5 (1= very dirty, 5= squeaky clean)
Other bathhouse notes: _____

Amenities: ○Pool ○Hot Tub ○Lodge/Game Room ○Adult Ctr ○Laundry ○Restaurant
○Shuffleboard ○Pickleball ○Mini Golf ○Pet-Friendly ○Dog Park
○Hiking ○Canoeing ○Fishing ○Horseback Riding ○Fitness Center

Other amenity notes:_____
_____

Management/Booking/Cancellation Notes: _____
_____

Any Campground Scenery?_____
_____

Maneuvering/Parking: ○Tight roads/turns ○Low-hanging trees ○Bad road conditions
Other parking notes:_____
_____
_____

Site-specific Notes: Site Number Stayed In: [_____]

Site Hookups: ○FHU ○W/E Only ○50 Amp ○30 Amp ○Dry Camping

RV Pad: ○Level ○Unlevel ○Concrete ○Rock ○Grass ○Dirt ○Other: _____

Site size: ○Tight ○Moderate ○Spacious ○Very large

Trees/Shade: ○Full Sun ○Some shade ○A lot of shade

Fire ring/pit? ○Y ○N Fires allowed? ○Y ○N Picnic table? ○Y ○N Nice view? ○Y ○N

Close to Amenities? ○Very Close ○Easy Walk ○Too far to walk

Noise: ○Quiet ○Light Road Noise ○Loud Road Noise ○Train ○Other:_____

Any wildlife, bugs, etc? _____

Other site-specific notes: _____

Local Area Notes:

Weather During Stay: ○Very Cold ○Cold ○Moderate ○Warm ○Hot

Other weather notes: _____

Nearby Sightseeing: _____

_____

Nearby Restaurants: _____

_____

Nearest Grocery Store: ○ 0-5 mi ○ 5-10 mi ○ 10-20mi ○ 20-30mi ○ 30+ mi

Other grocery or provisions notes: _____

Nearby places visited: _____

_____

_____

Visit/do next time: _____

_____

_____

Connectivity Notes: Wi-Fi: ○Y ○N Rating: 1 2 3 4 5 (1= horrible, 5= excellent)

Cellular signal: Verizon ▭▭▭ AT&T ▭▭▭ Sprint ▭▭▭ T-Mobile ▭▭▭ _____ ▭▭▭

Other Notes: _____

_____

Other notes: _____

_____

_____

_____

_____

_____

_____

_____

_____

_____

_____

Don't forget to add this Log Number to your reference section in the back!

Campground: _____ **Date(s):** ___ / ___ / ___

Location/Address/GPS: _____

Travel to Campground Miles: _____ Time: _____ Travel notes: _____

Cost(s): _____

General Campground/Park Notes:

Hookups: FHU: ○Some ○All ○W/E Only ○50&30 Amp ○30 Amp Only ○Dry Camping
○Dump Station   Other hookups notes:_____

Bathhouse: ○Flush Toilets ○Showers (○FREE ○Quarters) Enough Hot Water? ○Y ○N
Cleanliness: 1 2 3 4 5 (1= very dirty, 5= squeaky clean)
Other bathhouse notes: _____

Amenities: ○Pool ○Hot Tub ○Lodge/Game Room ○Adult Ctr ○Laundry ○Restaurant
○Shuffleboard ○Pickleball ○Mini Golf ○Pet-Friendly ○Dog Park
○Hiking ○Canoeing ○Fishing ○Horseback Riding ○Fitness Center

Other amenity notes:_____
_____

Management/Booking/Cancellation Notes: _____
_____

Any Campground Scenery?_____
_____

Maneuvering/Parking: ○Tight roads/turns ○Low-hanging trees ○Bad road conditions

Other parking notes:_____
_____
_____

Site-specific Notes: Site Number Stayed In: [_____]

Site Hookups: ○FHU   ○W/E Only   ○50 Amp   ○30 Amp   ○Dry Camping

RV Pad: ○Level ○Unlevel   ○Concrete ○Rock ○Grass ○Dirt ○Other: _____

Site size: ○Tight ○Moderate ○Spacious ○Very large

Trees/Shade: ○Full Sun ○Some shade ○A lot of shade

Fire ring/pit? ○Y ○N   Fires allowed? ○Y ○N   Picnic table? ○Y ○N   Nice view? ○Y ○N

Close to Amenities? ○Very Close ○Easy Walk ○Too far to walk

Noise: ○Quiet ○Light Road Noise ○Loud Road Noise ○Train ○Other:_____

Any wildlife, bugs, etc? _____

Other site-specific notes: _____

Local Area Notes:

Weather During Stay: ◯Very Cold ◯Cold ◯Moderate ◯Warm ◯Hot

Other weather notes: _____

Nearby Sightseeing: _____

_____

Nearby Restaurants: _____

_____

Nearest Grocery Store: ◯0-5 mi ◯5-10 mi ◯10-20mi ◯20-30mi ◯30+ mi

Other grocery or provisions notes: _____

Nearby places visited: _____

_____

_____

_____

Visit/do next time: _____

_____

_____

Connectivity Notes: Wi-Fi: ◯Y ◯N Rating: 1 2 3 4 5 (1= horrible, 5= excellent)

Cellular signal: Verizon ◻◻◻ AT&T ◻◻◻ Sprint ◻◻◻ T-Mobile ◻◻◻ _____ ◻◻◻

Other Notes: _____

_____

Other notes: _____

_____

_____

_____

_____

_____

_____

_____

_____

_____

_____

Campground: _____ **Date(s):**   /   /

Location/Address/GPS: _____

Travel to Campground Miles: _____ Time: _____ Travel notes: _____

Cost(s): _____

General Campground/Park Notes:

Hookups: FHU: ○Some ○All ○W/E Only   ○50&30 Amp ○30 Amp Only ○Dry Camping
　　　　　○Dump Station   Other hookups notes:_____

Bathhouse: ○ Flush Toilets ○Showers (○FREE ○Quarters) Enough Hot Water? ○Y ○N
　　　　　Cleanliness: 1 2 3 4 5 (1= very dirty, 5= squeaky clean)
　　　　　Other bathhouse notes: _____

Amenities: ○Pool ○Hot Tub ○Lodge/Game Room ○Adult Ctr ○Laundry ○Restaurant
　　　　　○Shuffleboard ○Pickleball ○Mini Golf ○Pet-Friendly ○ Dog Park
　　　　　○Hiking ○Canoeing ○Fishing ○Horseback Riding ○Fitness Center

Other amenity notes:_____
_____

Management/Booking/Cancellation Notes: _____
_____

Any Campground Scenery?_____
_____

Maneuvering/Parking: ○Tight roads/turns ○Low-hanging trees   ○Bad road conditions
Other parking notes:_____
_____
_____

Site-specific Notes:　　　　　**Site Number Stayed In:** [_____]

Site Hookups: ○FHU   ○W/E Only   ○50 Amp   ○30 Amp   ○Dry Camping

RV Pad: ○Level○Unlevel   ○Concrete ○Rock ○Grass ○Dirt ○Other: _____

Site size: ○Tight ○Moderate ○Spacious ○Very large

Trees/Shade: ○Full Sun ○Some shade ○A lot of shade

Fire ring/pit? ○Y○N   Fires allowed?○Y○N   Picnic table?○Y○N Nice view? ○Y ○N

Close to Amenities? ○Very Close ○Easy Walk ○Too far to walk

Noise: ○Quiet ○Light Road Noise ○Loud Road Noise ○Train ○Other:_____

Any wildlife, bugs, etc? _____

Other site-specific notes: _____

Local Area Notes:

Weather During Stay: ◯Very Cold ◯Cold ◯Moderate ◯Warm ◯Hot

Other weather notes: _____

Nearby Sightseeing: _____

_____

Nearby Restaurants: _____

_____

Nearest Grocery Store: ◯0-5 mi ◯5-10 mi ◯10-20mi ◯20-30mi ◯30+ mi

Other grocery or provisions notes: _____

Nearby places visited: _____

_____

_____

Visit/do next time: _____

_____

_____

Connectivity Notes: Wi-Fi: ◯Y ◯N Rating: 1 2 3 4 5 (1= horrible, 5= excellent)

Cellular signal: Verizon ▁▂▃ AT&T ▁▂▃ Sprint ▁▂▃ T-Mobile ▁▂▃ _____ ▁▂▃

Other Notes: _____

_____

Other notes: _____

_____

_____

_____

_____

_____

_____

_____

_____

_____

_____

Don't forget to add this Log Number to your reference section in the back!

Campground: _____ **Date(s):** ___ / ___ / ___

Location/Address/GPS: _____

Travel to Campground Miles: _____ Time: _____ Travel notes: _____

Cost(s): _____

General Campground/Park Notes:

Hookups: FHU: ○Some ○All ○W/E Only   ○50&30 Amp ○30 Amp Only ○Dry Camping
　　　　　　○Dump Station   Other hookups notes:_____

Bathhouse: ○ Flush Toilets ○Showers (○FREE ○Quarters) Enough Hot Water? ○Y ○N
　　　　　　Cleanliness: 1 2 3 4 5 (1= very dirty, 5= squeaky clean)
　　　　　　Other bathhouse notes: _____

Amenities: ○Pool ○Hot Tub ○Lodge/Game Room ○Adult Ctr ○Laundry ○Restaurant
　　　　　　○Shuffleboard ○Pickleball ○Mini Golf ○Pet-Friendly ○ Dog Park
　　　　　　○Hiking ○Canoeing ○Fishing ○Horseback Riding ○Fitness Center

Other amenity notes:_____
_____

Management/Booking/Cancellation Notes: _____
_____

Any Campground Scenery?_____
_____

Maneuvering/Parking: ○Tight roads/turns ○Low-hanging trees ○Bad road conditions
Other parking notes:_____
_____
_____

Site-specific Notes:　　　**Site Number Stayed In:** [_____]

Site Hookups: ○FHU ○W/E Only ○50 Amp ○30 Amp ○Dry Camping

RV Pad: ○Level ○Unlevel ○Concrete ○Rock ○Grass ○Dirt ○Other: _____

Site size: ○Tight ○Moderate ○Spacious ○Very large

Trees/Shade: ○Full Sun ○Some shade ○A lot of shade

Fire ring/pit? ○Y ○N Fires allowed? ○Y ○N Picnic table? ○Y ○N Nice view? ○Y ○N

Close to Amenities? ○Very Close ○Easy Walk ○Too far to walk

Noise: ○Quiet ○Light Road Noise ○Loud Road Noise ○Train ○Other:_____

Any wildlife, bugs, etc? _____

Other site-specific notes: _____

Local Area Notes:

Weather During Stay: ○Very Cold ○Cold ○Moderate ○Warm ○Hot

Other weather notes: _____

Nearby Sightseeing: _____

_____

Nearby Restaurants: _____

_____

Nearest Grocery Store: ○0-5 mi ○5-10 mi ○10-20mi ○20-30mi ○30+ mi

Other grocery or provisions notes: _____

Nearby places visited: _____

_____

_____

_____

Visit/do next time: _____

_____

_____

Connectivity Notes: Wi-Fi: ○Y ○N Rating: 1 2 3 4 5 (1= horrible, 5= excellent)

Cellular signal: Verizon ▢▢▢▢ AT&T ▢▢▢▢ Sprint ▢▢▢▢ T-Mobile ▢▢▢▢ _____ ▢▢▢▢

Other Notes: _____

_____

Other notes: _____

_____

_____

_____

_____

_____

_____

_____

_____

_____

_____

_____

Don't forget to add this Log Number to your reference section in the back!

Campground: _____ **Date(s):** ____ / ____ / ____

Location/Address/GPS: _____

Travel to Campground Miles: _____ Time: _____ Travel notes: _____

Cost(s): _____

General Campground/Park Notes:

Hookups: FHU: ○Some ○All ○W/E Only ○50&30 Amp ○30 Amp Only ○Dry Camping
○Dump Station Other hookups notes:_____

Bathhouse: ○Flush Toilets ○Showers (○FREE ○Quarters) Enough Hot Water? ○Y ○N
Cleanliness: 1 2 3 4 5 (1= very dirty, 5= squeaky clean)
Other bathhouse notes: _____

Amenities: ○Pool ○Hot Tub ○Lodge/Game Room ○Adult Ctr ○Laundry ○Restaurant
○Shuffleboard ○Pickleball ○Mini Golf ○Pet-Friendly ○Dog Park
○Hiking ○Canoeing ○Fishing ○Horseback Riding ○Fitness Center

Other amenity notes:_____
_____

Management/Booking/Cancellation Notes: _____
_____

Any Campground Scenery? _____
_____

Maneuvering/Parking: ○Tight roads/turns ○Low-hanging trees ○Bad road conditions
Other parking notes:_____
_____
_____

Site-specific Notes: Site Number Stayed In: [_____]

Site Hookups: ○FHU ○W/E Only ○50 Amp ○30 Amp ○Dry Camping

RV Pad: ○Level ○Unlevel ○Concrete ○Rock ○Grass ○Dirt ○Other: _____

Site size: ○Tight ○Moderate ○Spacious ○Very large

Trees/Shade: ○Full Sun ○Some shade ○A lot of shade

Fire ring/pit? ○Y ○N   Fires allowed? ○Y ○N   Picnic table? ○Y ○N   Nice view? ○Y ○N

Close to Amenities? ○Very Close ○Easy Walk ○Too far to walk

Noise: ○Quiet ○Light Road Noise ○Loud Road Noise ○Train ○Other:_____

Any wildlife, bugs, etc? _____

Other site-specific notes: _____

Local Area Notes:

Weather During Stay: ○Very Cold ○Cold ○Moderate ○Warm ○Hot

Other weather notes: _____

Nearby Sightseeing: _____

_____

Nearby Restaurants: _____

_____

Nearest Grocery Store: ○0-5 mi ○5-10 mi ○10-20mi ○20-30mi ○30+ mi

Other grocery or provisions notes: _____

Nearby places visited: _____

_____

_____

_____

Visit/do next time: _____

_____

_____

Connectivity Notes: Wi-Fi: ○Y ○N Rating: 1 2 3 4 5 (1= horrible, 5= excellent)

Cellular signal: Verizon ▯▯▯ AT&T ▯▯▯ Sprint ▯▯▯ T-Mobile ▯▯▯ _____ ▯▯▯

Other Notes: _____

_____

Other notes: _____

_____

_____

_____

_____

_____

_____

_____

_____

_____

_____

_____

_____

Don't forget to add this Log Number to your reference section in the back!

Campground: _____ **Date(s):** ____ / ____ / ____

Location/Address/GPS: _____

Travel to Campground Miles: _____ Time: _____ Travel notes: _____

Cost(s): _____

General Campground/Park Notes:

Hookups: FHU: ○Some ○All ○W/E Only ○50&30 Amp ○30 Amp Only ○Dry Camping
　　　　　○Dump Station　Other hookups notes:_____

Bathhouse: ○Flush Toilets ○Showers (○FREE ○Quarters)　Enough Hot Water? ○Y ○N
　　　　　Cleanliness: 1 2 3 4 5 (1= very dirty, 5= squeaky clean)
　　　　　Other bathhouse notes: _____

Amenities: ○Pool ○Hot Tub ○Lodge/Game Room ○Adult Ctr ○Laundry ○Restaurant
　　　　　○Shuffleboard ○Pickleball ○Mini Golf ○Pet-Friendly ○Dog Park
　　　　　○Hiking ○Canoeing ○Fishing ○Horseback Riding ○Fitness Center

Other amenity notes:_____
_____

Management/Booking/Cancellation Notes: _____
_____

Any Campground Scenery? _____
_____

Maneuvering/Parking: ○Tight roads/turns ○Low-hanging trees ○Bad road conditions
Other parking notes:_____
_____
_____

Site-specific Notes:　　　　**Site Number Stayed In:** ⬚

Site Hookups: ○FHU　○W/E Only　○50 Amp　○30 Amp　○Dry Camping

RV Pad: ○Level ○Unlevel　○Concrete ○Rock ○Grass ○Dirt ○Other: _____

Site size: ○Tight ○Moderate ○Spacious ○Very large

Trees/Shade: ○Full Sun ○Some shade ○A lot of shade

Fire ring/pit? ○Y ○N　Fires allowed? ○Y ○N　Picnic table? ○Y ○N　Nice view? ○Y ○N

Close to Amenities? ○Very Close ○Easy Walk ○Too far to walk

Noise: ○Quiet ○Light Road Noise ○Loud Road Noise ○Train ○Other:_____

Any wildlife, bugs, etc? _____

Other site-specific notes: _____

Local Area Notes:

Weather During Stay: ○Very Cold ○Cold ○Moderate ○Warm ○Hot

Other weather notes: _____

Nearby Sightseeing: _____

_____

Nearby Restaurants: _____

_____

Nearest Grocery Store: ○ 0-5 mi ○5-10 mi ○10-20mi ○ 20-30mi ○ 30+ mi

Other grocery or provisions notes: _____

Nearby places visited: _____

_____

_____

_____

Visit/do next time: _____

_____

_____

Connectivity Notes: Wi-Fi: ○Y ○N   Rating: 1 2 3 4 5 (1= horrible, 5= excellent)

Cellular signal: Verizon ▯▯▯ AT&T ▯▯▯ Sprint ▯▯▯ T-Mobile ▯▯▯ _____ ▯▯▯

Other Notes: _____

_____

Other notes: _____

_____

_____

_____

_____

_____

_____

_____

_____

_____

_____

Campground: _____ **Date(s):**   /   /

Location/Address/GPS: _____

Travel to Campground Miles: _____ Time: _____ Travel notes: _____

Cost(s): _____

General Campground/Park Notes:

Hookups: FHU: ○Some ○All ○W/E Only   ○50&30 Amp ○30 Amp Only ○Dry Camping
○Dump Station   Other hookups notes:_____

Bathhouse: ○Flush Toilets ○Showers (○FREE ○Quarters) Enough Hot Water? ○Y ○N
Cleanliness: 1 2 3 4 5 (1= very dirty, 5= squeaky clean)
Other bathhouse notes: _____

Amenities: ○Pool ○Hot Tub ○Lodge/Game Room ○Adult Ctr ○Laundry ○Restaurant
○Shuffleboard ○Pickleball ○Mini Golf ○Pet-Friendly ○ Dog Park
○Hiking ○Canoeing ○Fishing ○Horseback Riding ○Fitness Center

Other amenity notes:_____
_____

Management/Booking/Cancellation Notes: _____
_____

Any Campground Scenery?_____
_____

Maneuvering/Parking: ○Tight roads/turns ○Low-hanging trees   ○Bad road conditions
Other parking notes:_____
_____
_____

Site-specific Notes: Site Number Stayed In:[_____]

Site Hookups: ○FHU   ○W/E Only   ○50 Amp   ○30 Amp   ○Dry Camping

RV Pad: ○Level○Unlevel   ○Concrete ○Rock ○Grass ○Dirt ○Other: _____

Site size: ○Tight ○Moderate ○Spacious ○Very large

Trees/Shade: ○Full Sun ○Some shade ○A lot of shade

Fire ring/pit? ○Y○N   Fires allowed?○Y○N   Picnic table?○Y○N   Nice view? ○Y ○N

Close to Amenities? ○Very Close ○Easy Walk ○Too far to walk

Noise: ○Quiet ○Light Road Noise ○Loud Road Noise ○Train ○Other:_____

Any wildlife, bugs, etc? _____

Other site-specific notes: _____

Local Area Notes:

Weather During Stay: ⭕Very Cold ⭕Cold ⭕Moderate ⭕Warm ⭕Hot

Other weather notes: _____

Nearby Sightseeing: _____

_____

Nearby Restaurants: _____

_____

Nearest Grocery Store: ⭕0-5 mi ⭕5-10 mi ⭕10-20mi ⭕20-30mi ⭕30+ mi

Other grocery or provisions notes: _____

Nearby places visited: _____

_____

_____

_____

Visit/do next time: _____

_____

_____

Connectivity Notes: Wi-Fi: ⭕Y ⭕N   Rating: 1 2 3 4 5 (1= horrible, 5= excellent)

Cellular signal: Verizon ▯▯▯ AT&T ▯▯▯ Sprint ▯▯▯ T-Mobile ▯▯▯ _____ ▯▯▯

Other Notes: _____

_____

Other notes: _____

_____

_____

_____

_____

_____

_____

_____

_____

_____

_____

_____

Campground: _____ **Date(s):**   /   /

Location/Address/GPS: _____

Travel to Campground Miles: _____ Time: _____ Travel notes: _____

Cost(s): _____

General Campground/Park Notes:

Hookups: FHU: ○Some ○All ○W/E Only   ○50&30 Amp ○30 Amp Only ○Dry Camping
○Dump Station   Other hookups notes:_____

Bathhouse: ○Flush Toilets   ○Showers (○FREE ○Quarters)   Enough Hot Water? ○Y ○N
Cleanliness: 1 2 3 4 5 (1= very dirty, 5= squeaky clean)
Other bathhouse notes: _____

Amenities: ○Pool ○Hot Tub ○Lodge/Game Room ○Adult Ctr ○Laundry ○Restaurant
○Shuffleboard ○Pickleball ○Mini Golf ○Pet-Friendly ○Dog Park
○Hiking ○Canoeing ○Fishing ○Horseback Riding ○Fitness Center

Other amenity notes:_____
_____

Management/Booking/Cancellation Notes: _____
_____

Any Campground Scenery?_____
_____

Maneuvering/Parking: ○Tight roads/turns ○Low-hanging trees   ○Bad road conditions
Other parking notes:_____
_____
_____

Site-specific Notes: **Site Number Stayed In:** [_____]

Site Hookups: ○FHU   ○W/E Only   ○50 Amp   ○30 Amp   ○Dry Camping

RV Pad: ○Level○Unlevel   ○Concrete ○Rock ○Grass ○Dirt ○Other: _____

Site size: ○Tight ○Moderate ○Spacious ○Very large

Trees/Shade: ○Full Sun ○Some shade ○A lot of shade

Fire ring/pit? ○Y○N   Fires allowed?○Y ○N   Picnic table?○Y○N Nice view? ○Y ○N

Close to Amenities? ○Very Close ○Easy Walk ○Too far to walk

Noise: ○Quiet ○Light Road Noise ○Loud Road Noise ○Train ○Other:_____

Any wildlife, bugs, etc? _____

Other site-specific notes: _____

Local Area Notes:

Weather During Stay: ○Very Cold ○Cold ○Moderate ○Warm ○Hot

Other weather notes: _____

Nearby Sightseeing: _____

_____

Nearby Restaurants: _____

_____

Nearest Grocery Store: ○ 0-5 mi ○ 5-10 mi ○ 10-20mi ○ 20-30mi ○ 30+ mi

Other grocery or provisions notes: _____

Nearby places visited: _____

_____

_____

_____

Visit/do next time: _____

_____

_____

Connectivity Notes: Wi-Fi: ○Y ○N Rating: 1 2 3 4 5 (1= horrible, 5= excellent)

Cellular signal: Verizon ▫▫▫ AT&T ▫▫▫ Sprint ▫▫▫ T-Mobile ▫▫▫ _____ ▫▫▫

Other Notes: _____

_____

Other notes: _____

_____

_____

_____

_____

_____

_____

_____

_____

_____

_____

Campground: _____ **Date(s):** ____ / ____ / ____

Location/Address/GPS: _____

Travel to Campground Miles: _____ Time: _____ Travel notes: _____

Cost(s): _____

General Campground/Park Notes:

Hookups: FHU: ○Some ○All ○W/E Only ○50&30 Amp ○30 Amp Only ○Dry Camping
○Dump Station Other hookups notes:_____

Bathhouse: ○ Flush Toilets ○Showers (○FREE ○Quarters) Enough Hot Water? ○Y ○N
Cleanliness: 1 2 3 4 5 (1= very dirty, 5= squeaky clean)
Other bathhouse notes: _____

Amenities: ○Pool ○Hot Tub ○Lodge/Game Room ○Adult Ctr ○Laundry ○Restaurant
○Shuffleboard ○Pickleball ○Mini Golf ○Pet-Friendly ○Dog Park
○Hiking ○Canoeing ○Fishing ○Horseback Riding ○Fitness Center

Other amenity notes:_____
_____

Management/Booking/Cancellation Notes: _____
_____

Any Campground Scenery?_____
_____

Maneuvering/Parking: ○Tight roads/turns ○Low-hanging trees ○Bad road conditions
Other parking notes:_____
_____
_____

Site-specific Notes: Site Number Stayed In: [_____]

Site Hookups: ○FHU ○W/E Only ○50 Amp ○30 Amp ○Dry Camping

RV Pad: ○Level○Unlevel ○Concrete ○Rock ○Grass ○Dirt ○Other: _____

Site size: ○Tight ○Moderate ○Spacious ○Very large

Trees/Shade: ○Full Sun ○ Some shade ○A lot of shade

Fire ring/pit? ○Y○N Fires allowed?○Y○N Picnic table?○Y○N Nice view? ○Y ○N

Close to Amenities? ○Very Close ○Easy Walk ○Too far to walk

Noise: ○Quiet ○Light Road Noise ○Loud Road Noise ○Train ○Other:_____

Any wildlife, bugs, etc? _____

Other site-specific notes: _____

Local Area Notes:

Weather During Stay: ○Very Cold ○Cold ○Moderate ○Warm ○Hot

Other weather notes: _____

Nearby Sightseeing: _____

_____

Nearby Restaurants: _____

_____

Nearest Grocery Store: ○ 0-5 mi ○5-10 mi ○10-20mi ○ 20-30mi ○ 30+ mi

Other grocery or provisions notes: _____

Nearby places visited: _____

_____

_____

Visit/do next time: _____

_____

_____

Connectivity Notes: Wi-Fi: ○Y ○N   Rating: 1 2 3 4 5 (1= horrible, 5= excellent)

Cellular signal: Verizon ▫▫▫ AT&T ▫▫▫ Sprint ▫▫▫ T-Mobile ▫▫▫ _____ ▫▫▫

Other Notes: _____

_____

Other notes: _____

_____

_____

_____

_____

_____

_____

_____

_____

_____

_____

_____

Don't forget to add this Log Number to your reference section in the back!

Campground: _____ **Date(s):** ___ / ___ / ___

Location/Address/GPS: _____

Travel to Campground Miles: _____ Time: _____ Travel notes: _____

Cost(s): _____

General Campground/Park Notes:

Hookups: FHU: ○Some ○All ○W/E Only ○50&30 Amp ○30 Amp Only ○Dry Camping
○Dump Station   Other hookups notes:_____

Bathhouse: ○Flush Toilets ○Showers (○FREE ○Quarters)   Enough Hot Water? ○Y ○N
Cleanliness: 1 2 3 4 5 (1= very dirty, 5= squeaky clean)
Other bathhouse notes: _____

Amenities: ○Pool ○Hot Tub ○Lodge/Game Room ○Adult Ctr ○Laundry ○Restaurant
○Shuffleboard ○Pickleball ○Mini Golf ○Pet-Friendly ○Dog Park
○Hiking ○Canoeing ○Fishing ○Horseback Riding ○Fitness Center

Other amenity notes:_____
_____

Management/Booking/Cancellation Notes: _____
_____

Any Campground Scenery?_____
_____

Maneuvering/Parking: ○Tight roads/turns ○Low-hanging trees ○Bad road conditions
Other parking notes:_____
_____
_____

Site-specific Notes: Site Number Stayed In: [_____]

Site Hookups: ○FHU   ○W/E Only   ○50 Amp   ○30 Amp   ○Dry Camping

RV Pad: ○Level ○Unlevel   ○Concrete ○Rock ○Grass ○Dirt ○Other: _____

Site size: ○Tight ○Moderate ○Spacious ○Very large

Trees/Shade: ○Full Sun ○Some shade ○A lot of shade

Fire ring/pit? ○Y ○N   Fires allowed? ○Y ○N   Picnic table? ○Y ○N Nice view? ○Y ○N

Close to Amenities? ○Very Close ○Easy Walk ○Too far to walk

Noise: ○Quiet ○Light Road Noise ○Loud Road Noise ○Train ○Other:_____

Any wildlife, bugs, etc? _____

Other site-specific notes: _____

Local Area Notes:

Weather During Stay: ◯Very Cold ◯Cold ◯Moderate ◯Warm ◯Hot

Other weather notes: _____

Nearby Sightseeing: _____

_____

Nearby Restaurants: _____

_____

Nearest Grocery Store: ◯0-5 mi ◯5-10 mi ◯10-20mi ◯20-30mi ◯30+ mi

Other grocery or provisions notes: _____

Nearby places visited: _____

_____

_____

_____

Visit/do next time: _____

_____

_____

Connectivity Notes: Wi-Fi: ◯Y ◯N Rating: 1 2 3 4 5 (1= horrible, 5= excellent)

Cellular signal: Verizon ▭ᵢₗ AT&T ▭ᵢₗ Sprint ▭ᵢₗ T-Mobile ▭ᵢₗ _____ ▭ᵢₗ

Other Notes: _____

_____

Other notes: _____

_____

_____

_____

_____

_____

_____

_____

_____

_____

_____

Don't forget to add this Log Number to your reference section in the back!

Campground: _____ **Date(s):** ___ / ___ / ___

Location/Address/GPS: _____

Travel to Campground Miles: _____ Time: _____ Travel notes: _____

Cost(s): _____

General Campground/Park Notes:

Hookups: FHU: ○Some ○All ○W/E Only ○50&30 Amp ○30 Amp Only ○Dry Camping
○Dump Station Other hookups notes:_____

Bathhouse: ○Flush Toilets ○Showers (○FREE ○Quarters) Enough Hot Water? ○Y ○N
Cleanliness: 1 2 3 4 5 (1= very dirty, 5= squeaky clean)
Other bathhouse notes: _____

Amenities: ○Pool ○Hot Tub ○Lodge/Game Room ○Adult Ctr ○Laundry ○Restaurant
○Shuffleboard ○Pickleball ○Mini Golf ○Pet-Friendly ○Dog Park
○Hiking ○Canoeing ○Fishing ○Horseback Riding ○Fitness Center

Other amenity notes:_____
_____

Management/Booking/Cancellation Notes: _____
_____

Any Campground Scenery? _____
_____

Maneuvering/Parking: ○Tight roads/turns ○Low-hanging trees ○Bad road conditions
Other parking notes:_____
_____
_____

Site-specific Notes: Site Number Stayed In: [_____]

Site Hookups: ○FHU ○W/E Only ○50 Amp ○30 Amp ○Dry Camping

RV Pad: ○Level ○Unlevel ○Concrete ○Rock ○Grass ○Dirt ○Other: _____

Site size: ○Tight ○Moderate ○Spacious ○Very large

Trees/Shade: ○Full Sun ○Some shade ○A lot of shade

Fire ring/pit? ○Y ○N Fires allowed? ○Y ○N Picnic table? ○Y ○N Nice view? ○Y ○N

Close to Amenities? ○Very Close ○Easy Walk ○Too far to walk

Noise: ○Quiet ○Light Road Noise ○Loud Road Noise ○Train ○Other:_____

Any wildlife, bugs, etc? _____

Other site-specific notes: _____

Local Area Notes:

Weather During Stay: ○Very Cold ○Cold ○Moderate ○Warm ○Hot

Other weather notes: _____

Nearby Sightseeing: _____

_____

Nearby Restaurants: _____

_____

Nearest Grocery Store: ○ 0-5 mi ○ 5-10 mi ○ 10-20mi ○ 20-30mi ○ 30+ mi

Other grocery or provisions notes: _____

Nearby places visited: _____

_____

_____

_____

Visit/do next time: _____

_____

_____

LOG NUMBER

24

Connectivity Notes: Wi-Fi: ○Y ○N Rating: 1 2 3 4 5 (1= horrible, 5= excellent)

Cellular signal: Verizon ▫▫▫ AT&T ▫▫▫ Sprint ▫▫▫ T-Mobile ▫▫▫ _____ ▫▫▫

Other Notes: _____

_____

Other notes: _____

_____

_____

_____

_____

_____

_____

_____

_____

_____

_____

Campground: _____ **Date(s):** ___ / ___ / ___

Location/Address/GPS: _____

Travel to Campground Miles: _____ Time: _____ Travel notes: _____

Cost(s): _____

General Campground/Park Notes:

Hookups: FHU: ○Some ○All ○W/E Only   ○50&30 Amp ○30 Amp Only ○Dry Camping
○Dump Station   Other hookups notes:_____

Bathhouse: ○Flush Toilets ○Showers (○FREE ○Quarters) Enough Hot Water? ○Y ○N
Cleanliness: 1 2 3 4 5 (1= very dirty, 5= squeaky clean)
Other bathhouse notes: _____

Amenities: ○Pool ○Hot Tub ○Lodge/Game Room ○Adult Ctr ○Laundry ○Restaurant
○Shuffleboard ○Pickleball ○Mini Golf ○Pet-Friendly ○Dog Park
○Hiking ○Canoeing ○Fishing ○Horseback Riding ○Fitness Center

Other amenity notes:_____
_____

Management/Booking/Cancellation Notes: _____
_____

Any Campground Scenery?_____
_____

Maneuvering/Parking: ○Tight roads/turns ○Low-hanging trees ○Bad road conditions
Other parking notes:_____
_____
_____

Site-specific Notes: Site Number Stayed In: [_____]

Site Hookups: ○FHU   ○W/E Only   ○50 Amp   ○30 Amp   ○Dry Camping

RV Pad: ○Level ○Unlevel   ○Concrete ○Rock ○Grass ○Dirt ○Other: _____

Site size: ○Tight ○Moderate ○Spacious ○Very large

Trees/Shade: ○Full Sun ○Some shade ○A lot of shade

Fire ring/pit? ○Y ○N   Fires allowed? ○Y ○N   Picnic table? ○Y ○N Nice view? ○Y ○N

Close to Amenities? ○Very Close ○Easy Walk ○Too far to walk

Noise: ○Quiet ○Light Road Noise ○Loud Road Noise ○Train ○Other:_____

Any wildlife, bugs, etc? _____

Other site-specific notes: _____

Local Area Notes:

Weather During Stay: ◯Very Cold ◯Cold ◯Moderate ◯Warm ◯Hot

Other weather notes: _____

Nearby Sightseeing: _____

_____

Nearby Restaurants: _____

_____

Nearest Grocery Store: ◯0-5 mi ◯5-10 mi ◯10-20mi ◯20-30mi ◯30+ mi

Other grocery or provisions notes: _____

Nearby places visited: _____

_____

_____

_____

Visit/do next time: _____

_____

_____

Connectivity Notes: Wi-Fi: ◯Y ◯N   Rating: 1 2 3 4 5 (1= horrible, 5= excellent)

Cellular signal: Verizon ᵈᵢᵢᵢ AT&T ᵈᵢᵢᵢ Sprint ᵈᵢᵢᵢ T-Mobile ᵈᵢᵢᵢ _____ ᵈᵢᵢᵢ

Other Notes: _____

_____

Other notes: _____

_____

_____

_____

_____

_____

_____

_____

_____

_____

_____

Don't forget to add this Log Number to your reference section in the back!

Campground: _____ **Date(s):** ___ / ___ / ___

Location/Address/GPS: _____

Travel to Campground Miles: _____ Time: _____ Travel notes: _____
Cost(s): _____

General Campground/Park Notes:

Hookups: FHU: ○Some ○All ○W/E Only ○50&30 Amp ○30 Amp Only ○Dry Camping
○Dump Station   Other hookups notes:_____

Bathhouse: ○Flush Toilets ○Showers (○FREE ○Quarters)   Enough Hot Water? ○Y ○N
Cleanliness: 1 2 3 4 5 (1= very dirty, 5= squeaky clean)
Other bathhouse notes: _____

Amenities: ○Pool ○Hot Tub ○Lodge/Game Room ○Adult Ctr ○Laundry ○Restaurant
○Shuffleboard ○Pickleball ○Mini Golf ○Pet-Friendly ○Dog Park
○Hiking ○Canoeing ○Fishing ○Horseback Riding ○Fitness Center

Other amenity notes:_____
_____

Management/Booking/Cancellation Notes: _____
_____

Any Campground Scenery?_____
_____

Maneuvering/Parking: ○Tight roads/turns ○Low-hanging trees ○Bad road conditions
Other parking notes:_____
_____
_____

Site-specific Notes: Site Number Stayed In: [_____]

Site Hookups: ○FHU ○W/E Only ○50 Amp ○30 Amp ○Dry Camping
RV Pad: ○Level ○Unlevel ○Concrete ○Rock ○Grass ○Dirt ○Other: _____
Site size: ○Tight ○Moderate ○Spacious ○Very large
Trees/Shade: ○Full Sun ○Some shade ○A lot of shade
Fire ring/pit? ○Y ○N   Fires allowed? ○Y ○N   Picnic table? ○Y ○N   Nice view? ○Y ○N
Close to Amenities? ○Very Close ○Easy Walk ○Too far to walk
Noise: ○Quiet ○Light Road Noise ○Loud Road Noise ○Train ○Other:_____
Any wildlife, bugs, etc? _____
Other site-specific notes: _____

Local Area Notes:

Weather During Stay: ◯Very Cold ◯Cold ◯Moderate ◯Warm ◯Hot

Other weather notes: _____

Nearby Sightseeing: _____

_____

Nearby Restaurants: _____

_____

Nearest Grocery Store: ◯ 0-5 mi ◯ 5-10 mi ◯ 10-20mi ◯ 20-30mi ◯ 30+ mi

Other grocery or provisions notes: _____

Nearby places visited: _____

_____

_____

_____

Visit/do next time: _____

_____

_____

LOG NUMBER

26

Connectivity Notes: Wi-Fi: ◯Y ◯N Rating: 1 2 3 4 5 (1= horrible, 5= excellent)

Cellular signal: Verizon ▫▯▯▮ AT&T ▫▯▯▮ Sprint ▫▯▯▮ T-Mobile ▫▯▯▮ _____ ▫▯▯▮

Other Notes: _____

_____

Other notes: _____

_____

_____

_____

_____

_____

_____

_____

_____

_____

_____

Don't forget to add this Log Number to your reference section in the back!

Campground: _____ **Date(s):**   /   /

Location/Address/GPS: _____

Travel to Campground Miles: _____ Time: _____ Travel notes: _____

Cost(s): _____

General Campground/Park Notes:

Hookups: FHU: ○Some ○All ○W/E Only   ○50&30 Amp ○30 Amp Only ○Dry Camping
        ○Dump Station   Other hookups notes:_____

Bathhouse: ○Flush Toilets ○Showers (○FREE ○Quarters) Enough Hot Water? ○Y ○N
        Cleanliness: 1 2 3 4 5 (1= very dirty, 5= squeaky clean)
        Other bathhouse notes: _____

Amenities: ○Pool ○Hot Tub ○Lodge/Game Room ○Adult Ctr ○Laundry ○Restaurant
        ○Shuffleboard ○Pickleball ○Mini Golf ○Pet-Friendly ○Dog Park
        ○Hiking ○Canoeing ○Fishing ○Horseback Riding ○Fitness Center

Other amenity notes:_____
_____

Management/Booking/Cancellation Notes: _____
_____

Any Campground Scenery?_____
_____

Maneuvering/Parking: ○Tight roads/turns ○Low-hanging trees ○Bad road conditions
Other parking notes:_____
_____
_____

Site-specific Notes: Site Number Stayed In: [_____]

Site Hookups: ○FHU   ○W/E Only   ○50 Amp   ○30 Amp   ○Dry Camping

RV Pad: ○Level○Unlevel   ○Concrete ○Rock ○Grass ○Dirt ○Other: _____

Site size: ○Tight ○Moderate ○Spacious ○Very large

Trees/Shade: ○Full Sun ○Some shade ○A lot of shade

Fire ring/pit? ○Y○N   Fires allowed?○Y○N   Picnic table?○Y○N Nice view? ○Y ○N

Close to Amenities? ○Very Close ○Easy Walk ○Too far to walk

Noise: ○Quiet ○Light Road Noise ○Loud Road Noise ○Train ○Other:_____

Any wildlife, bugs, etc? _____

Other site-specific notes: _____

Local Area Notes:

Weather During Stay: ○Very Cold ○Cold ○Moderate ○Warm ○Hot

Other weather notes: _____

Nearby Sightseeing: _____

_____

Nearby Restaurants: _____

_____

Nearest Grocery Store: ○0-5 mi ○5-10 mi ○10-20mi ○20-30mi ○30+ mi

Other grocery or provisions notes:_____

Nearby places visited:_____

_____

_____

_____

Visit/do next time:_____

_____

_____

Connectivity Notes: Wi-Fi: ○Y ○N Rating: 1 2 3 4 5 (1= horrible, 5= excellent)

Cellular signal: Verizon ▁▃▅▇ AT&T ▁▃▅▇ Sprint ▁▃▅▇ T-Mobile ▁▃▅▇ _____ ▁▃▅▇

Other Notes: _____

_____

Other notes:_____

_____

_____

_____

_____

_____

_____

_____

_____

_____

_____

_____

_____

Don't forget to add this Log Number to your reference section in the back!

Campground: _____ **Date(s):**   /   /

Location/Address/GPS: _____

Travel to Campground Miles: _____ Time: _____ Travel notes: _____
Cost(s): _____

General Campground/Park Notes:

Hookups: FHU: ◯Some ◯All ◯W/E Only   ◯50&30 Amp ◯30 Amp Only ◯Dry Camping
　　　　　◯Dump Station   Other hookups notes:_____

Bathhouse: ◯ Flush Toilets ◯Showers (◯FREE ◯Quarters) Enough Hot Water? ◯Y ◯N
　　　　　Cleanliness: 1 2 3 4 5 (1= very dirty, 5= squeaky clean)
　　　　　Other bathhouse notes: _____

Amenities: ◯Pool ◯Hot Tub ◯Lodge/Game Room ◯Adult Ctr ◯Laundry ◯Restaurant
　　　　　◯Shuffleboard ◯Pickleball ◯Mini Golf ◯Pet-Friendly ◯ Dog Park
　　　　　◯Hiking ◯Canoeing ◯Fishing ◯Horseback Riding ◯Fitness Center

Other amenity notes:_____
_____

Management/Booking/Cancellation Notes: _____
_____

Any Campground Scenery?_____
_____

Maneuvering/Parking: ◯Tight roads/turns ◯Low-hanging trees ◯Bad road conditions
Other parking notes:_____
_____
_____

Site-specific Notes:　　　**Site Number Stayed In:** [_____]

Site Hookups: ◯FHU   ◯W/E Only   ◯50 Amp   ◯30 Amp   ◯Dry Camping

RV Pad: ◯Level◯Unlevel   ◯Concrete ◯Rock ◯Grass ◯Dirt ◯Other: _____

Site size: ◯Tight ◯Moderate ◯Spacious ◯Very large

Trees/Shade: ◯Full Sun ◯Some shade ◯A lot of shade

Fire ring/pit? ◯Y◯N   Fires allowed?◯Y◯N   Picnic table?◯Y◯N Nice view? ◯Y ◯N

Close to Amenities? ◯Very Close ◯Easy Walk ◯Too far to walk

Noise: ◯Quiet ◯Light Road Noise ◯Loud Road Noise ◯Train ◯Other:_____

Any wildlife, bugs, etc? _____

Other site-specific notes: _____

Local Area Notes:

LOG NUMBER **28**

Weather During Stay: ◯Very Cold ◯Cold ◯Moderate ◯Warm ◯Hot

Other weather notes: ______

Nearby Sightseeing: ______

Nearby Restaurants: ______

Nearest Grocery Store: ◯0-5 mi ◯5-10 mi ◯10-20mi ◯20-30mi ◯30+ mi

Other grocery or provisions notes: ______

Nearby places visited: ______

Visit/do next time: ______

Connectivity Notes: Wi-Fi: ◯Y ◯N Rating: 1 2 3 4 5 (1= horrible, 5= excellent)

Cellular signal: Verizon AT&T Sprint T-Mobile ______

Other Notes: ______

Other notes: ______

Don't forget to add this Log Number to your reference section in the back!

Campground: _____ **Date(s):**   /   /

Location/Address/GPS: _____

Travel to Campground Miles: _____ Time: _____ Travel notes: _____
Cost(s): _____

General Campground/Park Notes:

Hookups: FHU: ○Some ○All ○W/E Only   ○50&30 Amp ○30 Amp Only ○Dry Camping
         ○Dump Station   Other hookups notes:_____

Bathhouse: ○ Flush Toilets ○Showers (○FREE ○Quarters) Enough Hot Water? ○Y ○N
         Cleanliness: 1 2 3 4 5 (1= very dirty, 5= squeaky clean)
         Other bathhouse notes: _____

Amenities: ○Pool ○Hot Tub ○Lodge/Game Room ○Adult Ctr ○Laundry ○Restaurant
         ○Shuffleboard ○Pickleball ○Mini Golf ○Pet-Friendly ○Dog Park
         ○Hiking ○Canoeing ○Fishing ○Horseback Riding ○Fitness Center

Other amenity notes:_____
_____

Management/Booking/Cancellation Notes: _____
_____

Any Campground Scenery?_____
_____

Maneuvering/Parking: ○Tight roads/turns ○Low-hanging trees ○Bad road conditions
Other parking notes:_____
_____
_____

Site-specific Notes: Site Number Stayed In: [   ]

Site Hookups: ○FHU   ○W/E Only   ○50 Amp   ○30 Amp   ○Dry Camping

RV Pad: ○Level○Unlevel   ○Concrete ○Rock ○Grass ○Dirt ○Other: _____

Site size: ○Tight ○Moderate ○Spacious ○Very large

Trees/Shade: ○Full Sun ○Some shade ○A lot of shade

Fire ring/pit? ○Y○N   Fires allowed?○Y○N   Picnic table?○Y○N   Nice view? ○Y ○N

Close to Amenities? ○Very Close ○Easy Walk ○Too far to walk

Noise: ○Quiet ○Light Road Noise ○Loud Road Noise ○Train ○Other:_____

Any wildlife, bugs, etc? _____

Other site-specific notes: _____

Local Area Notes:

Weather During Stay: ○Very Cold ○Cold ○Moderate ○Warm ○Hot

LOG NUMBER
29

Other weather notes: _____

Nearby Sightseeing: _____

_____

Nearby Restaurants: _____

_____

Nearest Grocery Store: ○0-5 mi ○5-10 mi ○10-20mi ○20-30mi ○30+ mi

Other grocery or provisions notes: _____

Nearby places visited: _____

_____

_____

_____

Visit/do next time: _____

_____

_____

Connectivity Notes: Wi-Fi: ○Y ○N Rating: 1 2 3 4 5 (1= horrible, 5= excellent)

Cellular signal: Verizon ▯▯▯ AT&T ▯▯▯ Sprint ▯▯▯ T-Mobile ▯▯▯ _____ ▯▯▯

Other Notes: _____

_____

Other notes: _____

_____

_____

_____

_____

_____

_____

_____

_____

_____

_____

Don't forget to add this Log Number to your reference section in the back!

Campground: _____ **Date(s):**   /   /

Location/Address/GPS: _____

Travel to Campground Miles: _____ Time: _____ Travel notes: _____

Cost(s): _____

General Campground/Park Notes:

Hookups: FHU: ○Some ○All ○W/E Only   ○50&30 Amp ○30 Amp Only ○Dry Camping
○Dump Station   Other hookups notes:_____

Bathhouse: ○ Flush Toilets ○Showers (○FREE ○Quarters) Enough Hot Water? ○Y ○N
Cleanliness: 1 2 3 4 5 (1= very dirty, 5= squeaky clean)
Other bathhouse notes: _____

Amenities: ○Pool ○Hot Tub ○Lodge/Game Room ○Adult Ctr ○Laundry ○Restaurant
○Shuffleboard ○Pickleball ○Mini Golf ○Pet-Friendly ○Dog Park
○Hiking ○Canoeing ○Fishing ○Horseback Riding ○Fitness Center

Other amenity notes:_____
_____

Management/Booking/Cancellation Notes: _____
_____

Any Campground Scenery?_____
_____

Maneuvering/Parking: ○Tight roads/turns ○Low-hanging trees   ○Bad road conditions
Other parking notes:_____
_____
_____

Site-specific Notes: Site Number Stayed In: [_____]

Site Hookups: ○FHU   ○W/E Only   ○50 Amp   ○30 Amp   ○Dry Camping

RV Pad: ○Level○Unlevel   ○Concrete ○Rock ○Grass ○Dirt ○Other: _____

Site size: ○Tight ○Moderate ○Spacious ○Very large

Trees/Shade: ○Full Sun○Some shade ○A lot of shade

Fire ring/pit? ○Y○N   Fires allowed?○Y○N   Picnic table?○Y○N   Nice view? ○Y ○N

Close to Amenities? ○Very Close ○Easy Walk ○Too far to walk

Noise: ○Quiet ○Light Road Noise ○Loud Road Noise   ○Train ○Other:_____

Any wildlife, bugs, etc? _____

Other site-specific notes: _____

Local Area Notes:

Weather During Stay: ◯Very Cold ◯Cold ◯Moderate ◯Warm ◯Hot

Other weather notes: _____

Nearby Sightseeing: _____

_____

Nearby Restaurants: _____

_____

Nearest Grocery Store: ◯ 0-5 mi ◯ 5-10 mi ◯ 10-20mi ◯ 20-30mi ◯ 30+ mi

Other grocery or provisions notes: _____

Nearby places visited: _____

_____

_____

_____

Visit/do next time: _____

_____

_____

Connectivity Notes: Wi-Fi: ◯Y ◯N   Rating: 1 2 3 4 5 (1= horrible, 5= excellent)

Cellular signal: Verizon ▯▯▯ AT&T ▯▯▯ Sprint ▯▯▯ T-Mobile ▯▯▯ _____ ▯▯▯

Other Notes: _____

_____

Other notes: _____

_____

_____

_____

_____

_____

_____

_____

_____

_____

_____

Don't forget to add this Log Number to your reference section in the back!

Campground: _____ **Date(s):** ___ / ___ / ___

Location/Address/GPS: _____

Travel to Campground Miles: _____ Time: _____ Travel notes: _____

Cost(s): _____

General Campground/Park Notes:

Hookups: FHU: ○Some ○All ○W/E Only ○50&30 Amp ○30 Amp Only ○Dry Camping
　　　　　○Dump Station　Other hookups notes:_____

Bathhouse: ○ Flush Toilets ○Showers (○FREE ○Quarters)　Enough Hot Water? ○Y ○N
　　　　　　Cleanliness: 1 2 3 4 5 (1= very dirty, 5= squeaky clean)
　　　　　　Other bathhouse notes: _____

Amenities: ○Pool ○Hot Tub ○Lodge/Game Room ○Adult Ctr ○Laundry ○Restaurant
　　　　　　○Shuffleboard ○Pickleball ○Mini Golf ○Pet-Friendly ○Dog Park
　　　　　　○Hiking ○Canoeing ○Fishing ○Horseback Riding ○Fitness Center

Other amenity notes:_____
_____

Management/Booking/Cancellation Notes: _____
_____

Any Campground Scenery?_____
_____

Maneuvering/Parking: ○Tight roads/turns ○Low-hanging trees ○Bad road conditions

Other parking notes:_____
_____
_____

Site-specific Notes:　　　　**Site Number Stayed In:** [_____]

Site Hookups: ○FHU ○W/E Only ○50 Amp ○30 Amp ○Dry Camping

RV Pad: ○Level ○Unlevel ○Concrete ○Rock ○Grass ○Dirt ○Other: _____

Site size: ○Tight ○Moderate ○Spacious ○Very large

Trees/Shade: ○Full Sun ○Some shade ○A lot of shade

Fire ring/pit? ○Y ○N　Fires allowed? ○Y ○N　Picnic table? ○Y ○N　Nice view? ○Y ○N

Close to Amenities? ○Very Close ○Easy Walk ○Too far to walk

Noise: ○Quiet ○Light Road Noise ○Loud Road Noise ○Train ○Other:_____

Any wildlife, bugs, etc? _____

Other site-specific notes: _____

Local Area Notes:

Weather During Stay: ◯Very Cold ◯Cold ◯Moderate ◯Warm ◯Hot

Other weather notes: _____

Nearby Sightseeing: _____

_____

Nearby Restaurants: _____

_____

Nearest Grocery Store: ◯0-5 mi ◯5-10 mi ◯10-20mi ◯20-30mi ◯30+ mi

Other grocery or provisions notes: _____

Nearby places visited: _____

_____

_____

_____

Visit/do next time: _____

_____

_____

Connectivity Notes: Wi-Fi: ◯Y ◯N Rating: 1 2 3 4 5 (1= horrible, 5= excellent)

Cellular signal: Verizon ▫▫▫▫ AT&T ▫▫▫▫ Sprint ▫▫▫▫ T-Mobile ▫▫▫▫ _____ ▫▫▫▫

Other Notes: _____

_____

Other notes: _____

_____

_____

_____

_____

_____

_____

_____

_____

_____

_____

Don't forget to add this Log Number to your reference section in the back!

Campground: _____ **Date(s):** ___ / ___ / ___

Location/Address/GPS: _____

Travel to Campground Miles: _____ Time: _____ Travel notes: _____

Cost(s): _____

General Campground/Park Notes:

Hookups: FHU: ○Some ○All ○W/E Only ○50&30 Amp ○30 Amp Only ○Dry Camping
○Dump Station Other hookups notes:_____

Bathhouse: ○Flush Toilets ○Showers (○FREE ○Quarters) Enough Hot Water? ○Y ○N
Cleanliness: 1 2 3 4 5 (1= very dirty, 5= squeaky clean)
Other bathhouse notes: _____

Amenities: ○Pool ○Hot Tub ○Lodge/Game Room ○Adult Ctr ○Laundry ○Restaurant
○Shuffleboard ○Pickleball ○Mini Golf ○Pet-Friendly ○Dog Park
○Hiking ○Canoeing ○Fishing ○Horseback Riding ○Fitness Center

Other amenity notes:_____
_____

Management/Booking/Cancellation Notes: _____
_____

Any Campground Scenery?_____
_____

Maneuvering/Parking: ○Tight roads/turns ○Low-hanging trees ○Bad road conditions
Other parking notes:_____
_____
_____

Site-specific Notes: **Site Number Stayed In:** [_____]

Site Hookups: ○FHU ○W/E Only ○50 Amp ○30 Amp ○Dry Camping

RV Pad: ○Level ○Unlevel ○Concrete ○Rock ○Grass ○Dirt ○Other: _____

Site size: ○Tight ○Moderate ○Spacious ○Very large

Trees/Shade: ○Full Sun ○Some shade ○A lot of shade

Fire ring/pit? ○Y ○N Fires allowed? ○Y ○N Picnic table? ○Y ○N Nice view? ○Y ○N

Close to Amenities? ○Very Close ○Easy Walk ○Too far to walk

Noise: ○Quiet ○Light Road Noise ○Loud Road Noise ○Train ○Other:_____

Any wildlife, bugs, etc? _____

Other site-specific notes: _____

Local Area Notes:

Weather During Stay: ○Very Cold ○Cold ○Moderate ○Warm ○Hot

Other weather notes:_____

Nearby Sightseeing:_____

_____

Nearby Restaurants:_____

_____

Nearest Grocery Store: ○0-5 mi ○5-10 mi ○10-20mi ○20-30mi ○30+ mi

Other grocery or provisions notes:_____

Nearby places visited:_____

_____

_____

Visit/do next time:_____

_____

_____

Connectivity Notes: Wi-Fi: ○Y ○N Rating: 1 2 3 4 5 (1= horrible, 5= excellent)

Cellular signal: Verizon ⬚⬚⬚ AT&T ⬚⬚⬚ Sprint ⬚⬚⬚ T-Mobile ⬚⬚⬚ _____ ⬚⬚⬚

Other Notes:_____

_____

Other notes:_____

_____

_____

_____

_____

_____

_____

_____

_____

_____

_____

Don't forget to add this Log Number to your reference section in the back!

Campground: _____ **Date(s):** ____ / ____ / ____

Location/Address/GPS: _____

Travel to Campground Miles: _____ Time: _____ Travel notes: _____

Cost(s): _____

General Campground/Park Notes:

Hookups: FHU: ○Some ○All ○W/E Only ○50&30 Amp ○30 Amp Only ○Dry Camping
○Dump Station   Other hookups notes:_____

Bathhouse: ○Flush Toilets ○Showers (○FREE ○Quarters) Enough Hot Water? ○Y ○N
Cleanliness: 1 2 3 4 5 (1= very dirty, 5= squeaky clean)
Other bathhouse notes: _____

Amenities: ○Pool ○Hot Tub ○Lodge/Game Room ○Adult Ctr ○Laundry ○Restaurant
○Shuffleboard ○Pickleball ○Mini Golf ○Pet-Friendly ○Dog Park
○Hiking ○Canoeing ○Fishing ○Horseback Riding ○Fitness Center

Other amenity notes:_____
_____

Management/Booking/Cancellation Notes: _____
_____

Any Campground Scenery?_____
_____

Maneuvering/Parking: ○Tight roads/turns ○Low-hanging trees ○Bad road conditions
Other parking notes:_____
_____
_____

Site-specific Notes: Site Number Stayed In: [_____]

Site Hookups: ○FHU ○W/E Only ○50 Amp ○30 Amp ○Dry Camping

RV Pad: ○Level ○Unlevel ○Concrete ○Rock ○Grass ○Dirt ○Other: _____

Site size: ○Tight ○Moderate ○Spacious ○Very large

Trees/Shade: ○Full Sun ○Some shade ○A lot of shade

Fire ring/pit? ○Y○N   Fires allowed?○Y○N   Picnic table?○Y○N   Nice view? ○Y ○N

Close to Amenities? ○Very Close ○Easy Walk ○Too far to walk

Noise: ○Quiet ○Light Road Noise ○Loud Road Noise ○Train ○Other:_____

Any wildlife, bugs, etc? _____

Other site-specific notes: _____

Local Area Notes:

Weather During Stay: ○ Very Cold ○ Cold ○ Moderate ○ Warm ○ Hot

Other weather notes: _____

Nearby Sightseeing: _____
_____

Nearby Restaurants: _____
_____

Nearest Grocery Store: ○ 0-5 mi ○ 5-10 mi ○ 10-20mi ○ 20-30mi ○ 30+ mi

Other grocery or provisions notes: _____

Nearby places visited: _____
_____
_____
_____

Visit/do next time: _____
_____
_____

Connectivity Notes: Wi-Fi: ○ Y ○ N   Rating: 1 2 3 4 5 (1= horrible, 5= excellent)

Cellular signal: Verizon ▭▯▯▯ AT&T ▭▯▯▯ Sprint ▭▯▯▯ T-Mobile ▭▯▯▯ _____ ▭▯▯▯

Other Notes: _____
_____

Other notes: _____
_____
_____
_____
_____
_____
_____
_____
_____
_____
_____
_____

Don't forget to add this Log Number to your reference section in the back!

Campground: _____ **Date(s):** ___ / ___ / ___

Location/Address/GPS: _____

Travel to Campground Miles: _____ Time: _____ Travel notes: _____

Cost(s): _____

General Campground/Park Notes:

Hookups: FHU: ○Some ○All ○W/E Only ○50&30 Amp ○30 Amp Only ○Dry Camping
○Dump Station   Other hookups notes:_____

Bathhouse: ○Flush Toilets ○Showers (○FREE ○Quarters)   Enough Hot Water? ○Y ○N
Cleanliness: 1 2 3 4 5 (1= very dirty, 5= squeaky clean)
Other bathhouse notes: _____

Amenities: ○Pool ○Hot Tub ○Lodge/Game Room ○Adult Ctr ○Laundry ○Restaurant
○Shuffleboard ○Pickleball ○Mini Golf ○Pet-Friendly ○Dog Park
○Hiking ○Canoeing ○Fishing ○Horseback Riding ○Fitness Center

Other amenity notes:_____
_____

Management/Booking/Cancellation Notes: _____
_____

Any Campground Scenery?_____
_____

Maneuvering/Parking: ○Tight roads/turns ○Low-hanging trees ○Bad road conditions
Other parking notes:_____
_____
_____

Site-specific Notes: **Site Number Stayed In:** [_____]

Site Hookups: ○FHU ○W/E Only ○50 Amp ○30 Amp ○Dry Camping

RV Pad: ○Level ○Unlevel ○Concrete ○Rock ○Grass ○Dirt ○Other: _____

Site size: ○Tight ○Moderate ○Spacious ○Very large

Trees/Shade: ○Full Sun ○Some shade ○A lot of shade

Fire ring/pit? ○Y ○N   Fires allowed? ○Y ○N   Picnic table? ○Y ○N   Nice view? ○Y ○N

Close to Amenities? ○Very Close ○Easy Walk ○Too far to walk

Noise: ○Quiet ○Light Road Noise ○Loud Road Noise ○Train ○Other:_____

Any wildlife, bugs, etc? _____

Other site-specific notes: _____

Local Area Notes:

Weather During Stay: ○Very Cold ○Cold ○Moderate ○Warm ○Hot

Other weather notes: _____

Nearby Sightseeing: _____

_____

Nearby Restaurants: _____

_____

Nearest Grocery Store: ○0-5 mi ○5-10 mi ○10-20mi ○20-30mi ○30+ mi

Other grocery or provisions notes: _____

Nearby places visited: _____

_____

_____

_____

Visit/do next time: _____

_____

_____

Connectivity Notes: Wi-Fi: ○Y ○N Rating: 1 2 3 4 5 (1= horrible, 5= excellent)

Cellular signal: Verizon ▮▮▮ AT&T ▮▮▮ Sprint ▮▮▮ T-Mobile ▮▮▮ _____ ▮▮▮

Other Notes: _____

_____

Other notes: _____

_____

_____

_____

_____

_____

_____

_____

_____

_____

_____

Campground: _____ **Date(s):** ___ / ___ / ___

Location/Address/GPS: _____

Travel to Campground Miles: _____ Time: _____ Travel notes: _____
Cost(s): _____

General Campground/Park Notes:

Hookups: FHU: ○Some ○All ○W/E Only ○50&30 Amp ○30 Amp Only ○Dry Camping
○Dump Station   Other hookups notes:_____

Bathhouse: ○Flush Toilets ○Showers (○FREE ○Quarters) Enough Hot Water? ○Y ○N
Cleanliness: 1 2 3 4 5 (1= very dirty, 5= squeaky clean)
Other bathhouse notes: _____

Amenities: ○Pool ○Hot Tub ○Lodge/Game Room ○Adult Ctr ○Laundry ○Restaurant
○Shuffleboard ○Pickleball ○Mini Golf ○Pet-Friendly ○Dog Park
○Hiking ○Canoeing ○Fishing ○Horseback Riding ○Fitness Center

Other amenity notes:_____
_____

Management/Booking/Cancellation Notes: _____
_____

Any Campground Scenery?_____
_____

Maneuvering/Parking: ○Tight roads/turns ○Low-hanging trees ○Bad road conditions
Other parking notes:_____
_____
_____

Site-specific Notes: **Site Number Stayed In:** [_____]

Site Hookups: ○FHU ○W/E Only ○50 Amp ○30 Amp ○Dry Camping
RV Pad: ○Level ○Unlevel ○Concrete ○Rock ○Grass ○Dirt ○Other: _____
Site size: ○Tight ○Moderate ○Spacious ○Very large
Trees/Shade: ○Full Sun ○Some shade ○A lot of shade
Fire ring/pit? ○Y ○N Fires allowed? ○Y ○N Picnic table? ○Y ○N Nice view? ○Y ○N
Close to Amenities? ○Very Close ○Easy Walk ○Too far to walk
Noise: ○Quiet ○Light Road Noise ○Loud Road Noise ○Train ○Other:_____
Any wildlife, bugs, etc? _____
Other site-specific notes: _____

Local Area Notes:

Weather During Stay: ⭘Very Cold ⭘Cold ⭘Moderate ⭘Warm ⭘Hot

Other weather notes: _____

Nearby Sightseeing: _____

_____

Nearby Restaurants: _____

_____

Nearest Grocery Store: ⭘0-5 mi ⭘5-10 mi ⭘10-20mi ⭘20-30mi ⭘30+ mi

Other grocery or provisions notes: _____

Nearby places visited: _____

_____

_____

_____

Visit/do next time: _____

_____

_____

Connectivity Notes: Wi-Fi: ⭘Y ⭘N Rating: 1 2 3 4 5 (1= horrible, 5= excellent)

Cellular signal: Verizon ▫▫▫ AT&T ▫▫▫ Sprint ▫▫▫ T-Mobile ▫▫▫ _____ ▫▫▫

Other Notes: _____

_____

Other notes: _____

_____

_____

_____

_____

_____

_____

_____

_____

_____

_____

Don't forget to add this Log Number to your reference section in the back!

Campground: _____ **Date(s):** ___ / ___ / ___

Location/Address/GPS: _____

Travel to Campground Miles: _____ Time: _____ Travel notes: _____

Cost(s): _____

General Campground/Park Notes:

Hookups: FHU: ○Some ○All ○W/E Only ○50&30 Amp ○30 Amp Only ○Dry Camping
○Dump Station Other hookups notes:_____

Bathhouse: ○Flush Toilets ○Showers (○FREE ○Quarters) Enough Hot Water? ○Y ○N
Cleanliness: 1 2 3 4 5 (1= very dirty, 5= squeaky clean)
Other bathhouse notes: _____

Amenities: ○Pool ○Hot Tub ○Lodge/Game Room ○Adult Ctr ○Laundry ○Restaurant
○Shuffleboard ○Pickleball ○Mini Golf ○Pet-Friendly ○Dog Park
○Hiking ○Canoeing ○Fishing ○Horseback Riding ○Fitness Center

Other amenity notes:_____
_____

Management/Booking/Cancellation Notes: _____
_____

Any Campground Scenery?_____
_____

Maneuvering/Parking: ○Tight roads/turns ○Low-hanging trees ○Bad road conditions
Other parking notes:_____
_____
_____

Site-specific Notes: Site Number Stayed In: [_____]

Site Hookups: ○FHU ○W/E Only ○50 Amp ○30 Amp ○Dry Camping

RV Pad: ○Level ○Unlevel ○Concrete ○Rock ○Grass ○Dirt ○Other: _____

Site size: ○Tight ○Moderate ○Spacious ○Very large

Trees/Shade: ○Full Sun ○Some shade ○A lot of shade

Fire ring/pit? ○Y ○N Fires allowed? ○Y ○N Picnic table? ○Y ○N Nice view? ○Y ○N

Close to Amenities? ○Very Close ○Easy Walk ○Too far to walk

Noise: ○Quiet ○Light Road Noise ○Loud Road Noise ○Train ○Other:_____

Any wildlife, bugs, etc? _____

Other site-specific notes: _____

Local Area Notes:

Weather During Stay: ○Very Cold ○Cold ○Moderate ○Warm ○Hot

Other weather notes: _____

Nearby Sightseeing: _____

_____

Nearby Restaurants: _____

_____

Nearest Grocery Store: ○0-5 mi ○5-10 mi ○10-20mi ○20-30mi ○30+ mi

Other grocery or provisions notes: _____

Nearby places visited: _____

_____

_____

_____

Visit/do next time: _____

_____

_____

Connectivity Notes: Wi-Fi: ○Y ○N Rating: 1 2 3 4 5 (1= horrible, 5= excellent)

Cellular signal: Verizon ▫▫▫ AT&T ▫▫▫ Sprint ▫▫▫ T-Mobile ▫▫▫ _____ ▫▫▫

Other Notes: _____

_____

Other notes: _____

_____

_____

_____

_____

_____

_____

_____

_____

_____

_____

Campground: _____ **Date(s):** ____ / ____ / ____

Location/Address/GPS: _____

Travel to Campground Miles: _____ Time: _____ Travel notes: _____

Cost(s): _____

General Campground/Park Notes:

Hookups: FHU: ○Some ○All ○W/E Only ○50&30 Amp ○30 Amp Only ○Dry Camping
  ○Dump Station   Other hookups notes:_____

Bathhouse: ○ Flush Toilets ○Showers (○FREE ○Quarters) Enough Hot Water? ○Y ○N
  Cleanliness: 1 2 3 4 5 (1= very dirty, 5= squeaky clean)
  Other bathhouse notes: _____

Amenities: ○Pool ○Hot Tub ○Lodge/Game Room ○Adult Ctr ○Laundry ○Restaurant
  ○Shuffleboard ○Pickleball ○ Mini Golf ○Pet-Friendly ○ Dog Park
  ○Hiking ○Canoeing ○Fishing ○Horseback Riding ○Fitness Center

Other amenity notes:_____
_____

Management/Booking/Cancellation Notes: _____
_____

Any Campground Scenery? _____
_____

Maneuvering/Parking: ○Tight roads/turns ○Low-hanging trees ○Bad road conditions
Other parking notes:_____
_____
_____

Site-specific Notes: Site Number Stayed In: [_____]

Site Hookups: ○FHU   ○W/E Only   ○50 Amp   ○30 Amp   ○Dry Camping

RV Pad: ○Level○Unlevel   ○Concrete ○Rock ○Grass ○Dirt ○Other: _____

Site size: ○Tight ○Moderate ○Spacious ○Very large

Trees/Shade: ○Full Sun ○ Some shade ○A lot of shade

Fire ring/pit? ○Y○N   Fires allowed?○Y○N   Picnic table?○Y○N Nice view? ○Y ○N

Close to Amenities? ○Very Close ○Easy Walk ○Too far to walk

Noise: ○Quiet ○Light Road Noise ○Loud Road Noise ○Train ○Other:_____

Any wildlife, bugs, etc? _____

Other site-specific notes: _____

Local Area Notes:

Weather During Stay: ○Very Cold ○Cold ○Moderate ○Warm ○Hot

Other weather notes: _____

Nearby Sightseeing: _____

_____

Nearby Restaurants: _____

_____

Nearest Grocery Store: ○0-5 mi ○5-10 mi ○10-20mi ○20-30mi ○30+ mi

Other grocery or provisions notes: _____

Nearby places visited: _____

_____

_____

Visit/do next time: _____

_____

_____

Connectivity Notes: Wi-Fi: ○Y ○N Rating: 1 2 3 4 5 (1= horrible, 5= excellent)

Cellular signal: Verizon ▮▮▮ AT&T ▮▮▮ Sprint ▮▮▮ T-Mobile ▮▮▮ _____ ▮▮▮

Other Notes: _____

_____

Other notes: _____

_____

_____

_____

_____

_____

_____

_____

_____

_____

_____

Don't forget to add this Log Number to your reference section in the back!

Campground: _____ **Date(s):** ___ / ___ / ___

Location/Address/GPS: _____

Travel to Campground Miles: _____ Time: _____ Travel notes: _____

Cost(s): _____

General Campground/Park Notes:

Hookups: FHU: ○Some ○All ○W/E Only ○50&30 Amp ○30 Amp Only ○Dry Camping
○Dump Station   Other hookups notes:_____

Bathhouse: ○ Flush Toilets ○Showers (○FREE ○Quarters) Enough Hot Water? ○Y ○N
Cleanliness: 1 2 3 4 5 (1= very dirty, 5= squeaky clean)
Other bathhouse notes: _____

Amenities: ○Pool ○Hot Tub ○Lodge/Game Room ○Adult Ctr ○Laundry ○Restaurant
○Shuffleboard ○Pickleball ○ Mini Golf ○Pet-Friendly ○ Dog Park
○Hiking ○Canoeing ○Fishing ○Horseback Riding ○Fitness Center

Other amenity notes:_____
_____

Management/Booking/Cancellation Notes: _____
_____

Any Campground Scenery?_____
_____

Maneuvering/Parking: ○Tight roads/turns ○Low-hanging trees ○Bad road conditions
Other parking notes:_____
_____
_____

Site-specific Notes: Site Number Stayed In: [_____]

Site Hookups: ○FHU ○W/E Only ○50 Amp ○30 Amp ○Dry Camping

RV Pad: ○Level ○Unlevel ○Concrete ○Rock ○Grass ○Dirt ○Other: _____

Site size: ○Tight ○Moderate ○Spacious ○Very large

Trees/Shade: ○Full Sun ○Some shade ○A lot of shade

Fire ring/pit? ○Y ○N   Fires allowed? ○Y ○N   Picnic table? ○Y ○N   Nice view? ○Y ○N

Close to Amenities? ○Very Close ○Easy Walk ○Too far to walk

Noise: ○Quiet ○Light Road Noise ○Loud Road Noise ○Train ○Other:_____

Any wildlife, bugs, etc? _____

Other site-specific notes: _____

Local Area Notes:

Weather During Stay: ○Very Cold ○Cold ○Moderate ○Warm ○Hot

Other weather notes:_____

Nearby Sightseeing:_____

_____

Nearby Restaurants:_____

_____

Nearest Grocery Store: ○0-5 mi ○5-10 mi ○10-20mi ○20-30mi ○30+ mi

Other grocery or provisions notes:_____

Nearby places visited:_____

_____

_____

_____

Visit/do next time:_____

_____

_____

Connectivity Notes: Wi-Fi: ○Y ○N Rating: 1 2 3 4 5 (1= horrible, 5= excellent)

Cellular signal: Verizon ▭ AT&T ▭ Sprint ▭ T-Mobile ▭ _____ ▭

Other Notes:_____

_____

Other notes:_____

_____

_____

_____

_____

_____

_____

_____

_____

_____

_____

Campground: _____ **Date(s):** ___ / ___ / ___

Location/Address/GPS: _____

Travel to Campground Miles: _____ Time: _____ Travel notes: _____

Cost(s): _____

General Campground/Park Notes:

Hookups: FHU: ○Some ○All ○W/E Only ○50&30 Amp ○30 Amp Only ○Dry Camping
　　　　○Dump Station　Other hookups notes:_____

Bathhouse: ○Flush Toilets ○Showers (○FREE ○Quarters)　Enough Hot Water? ○Y ○N
　　　　Cleanliness: 1　2　3　4　5　(1= very dirty, 5= squeaky clean)
　　　　Other bathhouse notes: _____

Amenities: ○Pool ○Hot Tub ○Lodge/Game Room ○Adult Ctr ○Laundry ○Restaurant
　　　　○Shuffleboard ○Pickleball ○Mini Golf ○Pet-Friendly ○Dog Park
　　　　○Hiking ○Canoeing ○Fishing ○Horseback Riding ○Fitness Center

Other amenity notes:_____
_____

Management/Booking/Cancellation Notes: _____
_____

Any Campground Scenery? _____
_____

Maneuvering/Parking: ○Tight roads/turns ○Low-hanging trees ○Bad road conditions
Other parking notes:_____
_____
_____

Site-specific Notes:　　　**Site Number Stayed In:** [_____]

Site Hookups: ○FHU ○W/E Only ○50 Amp ○30 Amp ○Dry Camping

RV Pad: ○Level ○Unlevel ○Concrete ○Rock ○Grass ○Dirt ○Other: _____

Site size: ○Tight ○Moderate ○Spacious ○Very large

Trees/Shade: ○Full Sun ○Some shade ○A lot of shade

Fire ring/pit? ○Y ○N　Fires allowed? ○Y ○N　Picnic table? ○Y ○N　Nice view? ○Y ○N

Close to Amenities? ○Very Close ○Easy Walk ○Too far to walk

Noise: ○Quiet ○Light Road Noise ○Loud Road Noise ○Train ○Other:_____

Any wildlife, bugs, etc? _____

Other site-specific notes: _____

Local Area Notes:

Weather During Stay: ◯Very Cold ◯Cold ◯Moderate ◯Warm ◯Hot

Other weather notes: _____

Nearby Sightseeing: _____

_____

Nearby Restaurants: _____

_____

Nearest Grocery Store: ◯0-5 mi ◯5-10 mi ◯10-20mi ◯20-30mi ◯30+ mi

Other grocery or provisions notes: _____

Nearby places visited: _____

_____

_____

_____

Visit/do next time: _____

_____

_____

Connectivity Notes: Wi-Fi: ◯Y ◯N Rating: 1 2 3 4 5 (1= horrible, 5= excellent)

Cellular signal: Verizon ▭ AT&T ▭ Sprint ▭ T-Mobile ▭ _____ ▭

Other Notes: _____

_____

Other notes: _____

_____

_____

_____

_____

_____

_____

_____

_____

_____

_____

_____

Don't forget to add this Log Number to your reference section in the back!

Campground: _____ **Date(s):** ___ / ___ / ___

Location/Address/GPS: _____

Travel to Campground Miles: _____ Time: _____ Travel notes: _____

Cost(s): _____

General Campground/Park Notes:

Hookups: FHU: ◯Some ◯All ◯W/E Only ◯50&30 Amp ◯30 Amp Only ◯Dry Camping
◯Dump Station   Other hookups notes:_____

Bathhouse: ◯ Flush Toilets ◯Showers (◯FREE ◯Quarters) Enough Hot Water? ◯Y ◯N
Cleanliness: 1 2 3 4 5 (1= very dirty, 5= squeaky clean)
Other bathhouse notes: _____

Amenities: ◯Pool ◯Hot Tub ◯Lodge/Game Room ◯Adult Ctr ◯Laundry ◯Restaurant
◯Shuffleboard ◯Pickleball ◯Mini Golf ◯Pet-Friendly ◯ Dog Park
◯Hiking ◯Canoeing ◯Fishing ◯Horseback Riding ◯Fitness Center

Other amenity notes:_____
_____

Management/Booking/Cancellation Notes: _____
_____

Any Campground Scenery?_____
_____

Maneuvering/Parking: ◯Tight roads/turns ◯Low-hanging trees ◯Bad road conditions
Other parking notes:_____
_____
_____

Site-specific Notes: **Site Number Stayed In:** [_____]

Site Hookups: ◯FHU ◯W/E Only ◯50 Amp ◯30 Amp ◯Dry Camping

RV Pad: ◯Level ◯Unlevel ◯Concrete ◯Rock ◯Grass ◯Dirt ◯Other: _____

Site size: ◯Tight ◯Moderate ◯Spacious ◯Very large

Trees/Shade: ◯Full Sun ◯Some shade ◯A lot of shade

Fire ring/pit? ◯Y ◯N Fires allowed? ◯Y ◯N Picnic table? ◯Y ◯N Nice view? ◯Y ◯N

Close to Amenities? ◯Very Close ◯Easy Walk ◯Too far to walk

Noise: ◯Quiet ◯Light Road Noise ◯Loud Road Noise ◯Train ◯Other:_____

Any wildlife, bugs, etc? _____

Other site-specific notes: _____

Local Area Notes:

Weather During Stay: ○Very Cold ○Cold ○Moderate ○Warm ○Hot

Other weather notes:_____

Nearby Sightseeing:_____

_____

Nearby Restaurants:_____

_____

Nearest Grocery Store: ○0-5 mi ○5-10 mi ○10-20mi ○20-30mi ○30+ mi

Other grocery or provisions notes:_____

Nearby places visited:_____

_____

_____

_____

Visit/do next time:_____

_____

_____

Connectivity Notes: Wi-Fi: ○Y ○N Rating: 1 2 3 4 5 (1= horrible, 5= excellent)

Cellular signal: Verizon ▫▯▯▯ AT&T ▫▯▯▯ Sprint ▫▯▯▯ T-Mobile ▫▯▯▯ _____ ▫▯▯▯

Other Notes:_____

_____

Other notes:_____

_____

_____

_____

_____

_____

_____

_____

_____

_____

_____

_____

Don't forget to add this Log Number to your reference section in the back!

Campground: _____ **Date(s):** ___ / ___ / ___

Location/Address/GPS: _____

Travel to Campground Miles: _____ Time: _____ Travel notes: _____

Cost(s): _____

General Campground/Park Notes:

Hookups: FHU: ○Some ○All ○W/E Only ○50&30 Amp ○30 Amp Only ○Dry Camping
○Dump Station Other hookups notes:_____

Bathhouse: ○Flush Toilets ○Showers (○FREE ○Quarters) Enough Hot Water? ○Y ○N
Cleanliness: 1 2 3 4 5 (1= very dirty, 5= squeaky clean)
Other bathhouse notes: _____

Amenities: ○Pool ○Hot Tub ○Lodge/Game Room ○Adult Ctr ○Laundry ○Restaurant
○Shuffleboard ○Pickleball ○Mini Golf ○Pet-Friendly ○Dog Park
○Hiking ○Canoeing ○Fishing ○Horseback Riding ○Fitness Center

Other amenity notes:_____
_____

Management/Booking/Cancellation Notes: _____
_____

Any Campground Scenery?_____
_____

Maneuvering/Parking: ○Tight roads/turns ○Low-hanging trees ○Bad road conditions
Other parking notes:_____
_____
_____

Site-specific Notes: Site Number Stayed In: [_____]

Site Hookups: ○FHU ○W/E Only ○50 Amp ○30 Amp ○Dry Camping

RV Pad: ○Level ○Unlevel ○Concrete ○Rock ○Grass ○Dirt ○Other: _____

Site size: ○Tight ○Moderate ○Spacious ○Very large

Trees/Shade: ○Full Sun ○Some shade ○A lot of shade

Fire ring/pit? ○Y ○N   Fires allowed? ○Y ○N   Picnic table? ○Y ○N   Nice view? ○Y ○N

Close to Amenities? ○Very Close ○Easy Walk ○Too far to walk

Noise: ○Quiet ○Light Road Noise ○Loud Road Noise ○Train ○Other:_____

Any wildlife, bugs, etc? _____

Other site-specific notes: _____

Local Area Notes:

Weather During Stay: ○Very Cold ○Cold ○Moderate ○Warm ○Hot

Other weather notes: _____

Nearby Sightseeing: _____

_____

Nearby Restaurants: _____

_____

Nearest Grocery Store: ○0-5 mi ○5-10 mi ○10-20mi ○20-30mi ○30+ mi

Other grocery or provisions notes: _____

Nearby places visited: _____

_____

_____

Visit/do next time: _____

_____

_____

Connectivity Notes: Wi-Fi: ○Y ○N Rating: 1 2 3 4 5 (1= horrible, 5= excellent)

Cellular signal: Verizon ▭◫◫ AT&T ▭◫◫ Sprint ▭◫◫ T-Mobile ▭◫◫ _____ ▭◫◫

Other Notes: _____

_____

Other notes: _____

_____

_____

_____

_____

_____

_____

_____

_____

_____

_____

Campground: _____ **Date(s):** ____ / ____ / ____

Location/Address/GPS: _____

Travel to Campground Miles: _____ Time: _____ Travel notes: _____

Cost(s): _____

General Campground/Park Notes:

Hookups: FHU: ○Some ○All ○W/E Only   ○50&30 Amp ○30 Amp Only ○Dry Camping
  ○Dump Station   Other hookups notes:_____

Bathhouse:○ Flush Toilets ○Showers (○FREE ○Quarters) Enough Hot Water? ○Y ○N
  Cleanliness: 1 2 3 4 5 (1= very dirty, 5= squeaky clean)
  Other bathhouse notes: _____

Amenities: ○Pool ○Hot Tub ○Lodge/Game Room ○Adult Ctr ○Laundry ○Restaurant
  ○Shuffleboard ○Pickleball ○ Mini Golf ○Pet-Friendly ○ Dog Park
  ○Hiking ○Canoeing ○Fishing ○Horseback Riding ○Fitness Center

Other amenity notes:_____
_____

Management/Booking/Cancellation Notes: _____
_____

Any Campground Scenery?_____
_____

Maneuvering/Parking: ○Tight roads/turns ○Low-hanging trees ○Bad road conditions
Other parking notes:_____
_____
_____

Site-specific Notes: Site Number Stayed In:[_____]

Site Hookups: ○FHU   ○W/E Only   ○50 Amp   ○30 Amp   ○Dry Camping

RV Pad: ○Level○Unlevel   ○Concrete ○Rock ○Grass ○Dirt ○Other: _____

Site size: ○Tight ○Moderate ○Spacious ○Very large

Trees/Shade: ○Full Sun○ Some shade ○A lot of shade

Fire ring/pit? ○Y○N   Fires allowed?○Y○N   Picnic table?○Y○N Nice view? ○Y ○N

Close to Amenities? ○Very Close ○Easy Walk ○Too far to walk

Noise: ○Quiet ○Light Road Noise ○Loud Road Noise ○Train ○Other:_____

Any wildlife, bugs, etc? _____

Other site-specific notes: _____

Local Area Notes:

Weather During Stay: ⭕Very Cold ⭕Cold ⭕Moderate ⭕Warm ⭕Hot

LOG NUMBER
42

Other weather notes: _____

Nearby Sightseeing: _____

_____

Nearby Restaurants: _____

_____

Nearest Grocery Store: ⭕0-5 mi ⭕5-10 mi ⭕10-20mi ⭕20-30mi ⭕30+ mi

Other grocery or provisions notes: _____

Nearby places visited: _____

_____

_____

Visit/do next time: _____

_____

_____

Connectivity Notes: Wi-Fi: ⭕Y ⭕N Rating: 1 2 3 4 5 (1= horrible, 5= excellent)

Cellular signal: Verizon ▁▃▅ AT&T ▁▃▅ Sprint ▁▃▅ T-Mobile ▁▃▅ _____ ▁▃▅

Other Notes: _____

_____

Other notes: _____

_____

_____

_____

_____

_____

_____

_____

_____

_____

_____

Don't forget to add this Log Number to your reference section in the back!

Campground: _____ **Date(s):** ___ / ___ / ___

Location/Address/GPS: _____

Travel to Campground Miles: _____ Time: _____ Travel notes: _____
Cost(s): _____

General Campground/Park Notes:

Hookups: FHU: ○Some ○All ○W/E Only ○50&30 Amp ○30 Amp Only ○Dry Camping
○Dump Station Other hookups notes:_____

Bathhouse: ○Flush Toilets ○Showers (○FREE ○Quarters) Enough Hot Water? ○Y ○N
Cleanliness: 1 2 3 4 5 (1= very dirty, 5= squeaky clean)
Other bathhouse notes: _____

Amenities: ○Pool ○Hot Tub ○Lodge/Game Room ○Adult Ctr ○Laundry ○Restaurant
○Shuffleboard ○Pickleball ○Mini Golf ○Pet-Friendly ○Dog Park
○Hiking ○Canoeing ○Fishing ○Horseback Riding ○Fitness Center

Other amenity notes:_____
_____

Management/Booking/Cancellation Notes: _____
_____

Any Campground Scenery?_____
_____

Maneuvering/Parking: ○Tight roads/turns ○Low-hanging trees ○Bad road conditions
Other parking notes:_____
_____
_____

Site-specific Notes: Site Number Stayed In: [_____]

Site Hookups: ○FHU ○W/E Only ○50 Amp ○30 Amp ○Dry Camping
RV Pad: ○Level ○Unlevel ○Concrete ○Rock ○Grass ○Dirt ○Other: _____
Site size: ○Tight ○Moderate ○Spacious ○Very large
Trees/Shade: ○Full Sun ○Some shade ○A lot of shade
Fire ring/pit? ○Y ○N Fires allowed? ○Y ○N Picnic table? ○Y ○N Nice view? ○Y ○N
Close to Amenities? ○Very Close ○Easy Walk ○Too far to walk
Noise: ○Quiet ○Light Road Noise ○Loud Road Noise ○Train ○Other:_____
Any wildlife, bugs, etc? _____
Other site-specific notes: _____

Local Area Notes:

Weather During Stay: ○Very Cold ○Cold ○Moderate ○Warm ○Hot

Other weather notes: _____

Nearby Sightseeing: _____

_____

Nearby Restaurants: _____

_____

Nearest Grocery Store: ○0-5 mi ○5-10 mi ○10-20mi ○20-30mi ○30+ mi

Other grocery or provisions notes: _____

Nearby places visited: _____

_____

_____

_____

Visit/do next time: _____

_____

_____

Connectivity Notes: Wi-Fi: ○Y ○N Rating: 1 2 3 4 5 (1= horrible, 5= excellent)

Cellular signal: Verizon ▢▢▢▢ AT&T ▢▢▢▢ Sprint ▢▢▢▢ T-Mobile ▢▢▢▢ _____ ▢▢▢▢

Other Notes: _____

_____

Other notes: _____

_____

_____

_____

_____

_____

_____

_____

_____

_____

_____

Don't forget to add this Log Number to your reference section in the back!

Campground: _____ **Date(s):** ___ / ___ / ___

Location/Address/GPS: _____

Travel to Campground Miles: _____ Time: _____ Travel notes: _____

Cost(s): _____

General Campground/Park Notes:

Hookups: FHU: ○Some ○All ○W/E Only ○50&30 Amp ○30 Amp Only ○Dry Camping
  ○Dump Station Other hookups notes:_____

Bathhouse: ○Flush Toilets ○Showers (○FREE ○Quarters) Enough Hot Water? ○Y ○N
  Cleanliness: 1 2 3 4 5 (1= very dirty, 5= squeaky clean)
  Other bathhouse notes: _____

Amenities: ○Pool ○Hot Tub ○Lodge/Game Room ○Adult Ctr ○Laundry ○Restaurant
  ○Shuffleboard ○Pickleball ○Mini Golf ○Pet-Friendly ○Dog Park
  ○Hiking ○Canoeing ○Fishing ○Horseback Riding ○Fitness Center

Other amenity notes:_____
_____

Management/Booking/Cancellation Notes: _____
_____

Any Campground Scenery?_____
_____

Maneuvering/Parking: ○Tight roads/turns ○Low-hanging trees ○Bad road conditions
Other parking notes:_____
_____
_____

Site-specific Notes: **Site Number Stayed In:** [_____]

Site Hookups: ○FHU ○W/E Only ○50 Amp ○30 Amp ○Dry Camping

RV Pad: ○Level ○Unlevel ○Concrete ○Rock ○Grass ○Dirt ○Other: _____

Site size: ○Tight ○Moderate ○Spacious ○Very large

Trees/Shade: ○Full Sun ○Some shade ○A lot of shade

Fire ring/pit? ○Y ○N Fires allowed? ○Y ○N Picnic table? ○Y ○N Nice view? ○Y ○N

Close to Amenities? ○Very Close ○Easy Walk ○Too far to walk

Noise: ○Quiet ○Light Road Noise ○Loud Road Noise ○Train ○Other:_____

Any wildlife, bugs, etc? _____

Other site-specific notes: _____

Local Area Notes:

Weather During Stay: ○Very Cold ○Cold ○Moderate ○Warm ○Hot

Other weather notes: _____

Nearby Sightseeing: _____

_____

Nearby Restaurants: _____

_____

Nearest Grocery Store: ○0-5 mi ○5-10 mi ○10-20mi ○20-30mi ○30+ mi

Other grocery or provisions notes: _____

Nearby places visited: _____

_____

_____

_____

Visit/do next time: _____

_____

_____

Connectivity Notes: Wi-Fi: ○Y ○N   Rating: 1 2 3 4 5 (1= horrible, 5= excellent)

Cellular signal: Verizon ▫▫▫ AT&T ▫▫▫ Sprint ▫▫▫ T-Mobile ▫▫▫ _____ ▫▫▫

Other Notes: _____

_____

Other notes: _____

_____

_____

_____

_____

_____

_____

_____

_____

_____

_____

Don't forget to add this Log Number to your reference section in the back!

Campground: _____ **Date(s):** ___ / ___ / ___

Location/Address/GPS: _____

Travel to Campground Miles: _____ Time: _____ Travel notes: _____

Cost(s): _____

General Campground/Park Notes:

Hookups: FHU: ○Some ○All ○W/E Only   ○50&30 Amp ○30 Amp Only ○Dry Camping
○Dump Station   Other hookups notes:_____

Bathhouse: ○Flush Toilets ○Showers (○FREE ○Quarters) Enough Hot Water? ○Y ○N
Cleanliness: 1 2 3 4 5 (1= very dirty, 5= squeaky clean)
Other bathhouse notes: _____

Amenities: ○Pool ○Hot Tub ○Lodge/Game Room ○Adult Ctr ○Laundry ○Restaurant
○Shuffleboard ○Pickleball ○Mini Golf ○Pet-Friendly ○ Dog Park
○Hiking ○Canoeing ○Fishing ○Horseback Riding ○Fitness Center

Other amenity notes:_____
_____

Management/Booking/Cancellation Notes: _____
_____

Any Campground Scenery? _____
_____

Maneuvering/Parking: ○Tight roads/turns ○Low-hanging trees ○Bad road conditions
Other parking notes:_____
_____
_____

Site-specific Notes: **Site Number Stayed In:** [_____]

Site Hookups: ○FHU ○W/E Only ○50 Amp ○30 Amp ○Dry Camping

RV Pad: ○Level ○Unlevel ○Concrete ○Rock ○Grass ○Dirt ○Other: _____

Site size: ○Tight ○Moderate ○Spacious ○Very large

Trees/Shade: ○Full Sun ○Some shade ○A lot of shade

Fire ring/pit? ○Y ○N Fires allowed? ○Y ○N Picnic table? ○Y ○N Nice view? ○Y ○N

Close to Amenities? ○Very Close ○Easy Walk ○Too far to walk

Noise: ○Quiet ○Light Road Noise ○Loud Road Noise ○Train ○Other:_____

Any wildlife, bugs, etc? _____

Other site-specific notes: _____

Local Area Notes:

Weather During Stay: ⬭Very Cold ⬭Cold ⬭Moderate ⬭Warm ⬭Hot

Other weather notes: _____

Nearby Sightseeing: _____

_____

Nearby Restaurants: _____

_____

Nearest Grocery Store: ⬭0-5 mi ⬭5-10 mi ⬭10-20mi ⬭20-30mi ⬭30+ mi

Other grocery or provisions notes: _____

Nearby places visited: _____

_____

_____

_____

Visit/do next time: _____

_____

_____

Connectivity Notes: Wi-Fi: ⬭Y ⬭N   Rating: 1 2 3 4 5 (1= horrible, 5= excellent)

Cellular signal: Verizon 📶 AT&T 📶 Sprint 📶 T-Mobile 📶 _____ 📶

Other Notes: _____

_____

Other notes: _____

_____

_____

_____

_____

_____

_____

_____

_____

_____

_____

Don't forget to add this Log Number to your reference section in the back!

Campground: _____ **Date(s):** ___ / ___ / ___

Location/Address/GPS: _____

Travel to Campground Miles: _____ Time: _____ Travel notes: _____

Cost(s): _____

General Campground/Park Notes:

Hookups: FHU: ○Some ○All ○W/E Only ○50&30 Amp ○30 Amp Only ○Dry Camping
○Dump Station   Other hookups notes:_____

Bathhouse: ○Flush Toilets ○Showers (○FREE ○Quarters)   Enough Hot Water? ○Y ○N
Cleanliness: 1 2 3 4 5 (1= very dirty, 5= squeaky clean)
Other bathhouse notes: _____

Amenities: ○Pool ○Hot Tub ○Lodge/Game Room ○Adult Ctr ○Laundry ○Restaurant
○Shuffleboard ○Pickleball ○Mini Golf ○Pet-Friendly ○Dog Park
○Hiking ○Canoeing ○Fishing ○Horseback Riding ○Fitness Center

Other amenity notes:_____
_____

Management/Booking/Cancellation Notes: _____
_____

Any Campground Scenery?_____
_____

Maneuvering/Parking: ○Tight roads/turns ○Low-hanging trees ○Bad road conditions
Other parking notes:_____
_____
_____

Site-specific Notes: Site Number Stayed In: [_____]

Site Hookups: ○FHU ○W/E Only ○50 Amp ○30 Amp ○Dry Camping

RV Pad: ○Level ○Unlevel ○Concrete ○Rock ○Grass ○Dirt ○Other: _____

Site size: ○Tight ○Moderate ○Spacious ○Very large

Trees/Shade: ○Full Sun ○Some shade ○A lot of shade

Fire ring/pit? ○Y ○N   Fires allowed? ○Y ○N   Picnic table? ○Y ○N   Nice view? ○Y ○N

Close to Amenities? ○Very Close ○Easy Walk ○Too far to walk

Noise: ○Quiet ○Light Road Noise ○Loud Road Noise ○Train ○Other:_____

Any wildlife, bugs, etc? _____

Other site-specific notes: _____

Local Area Notes:

Weather During Stay: ○Very Cold ○Cold ○Moderate ○Warm ○Hot

Other weather notes: _____

Nearby Sightseeing: _____

_____

Nearby Restaurants: _____

_____

Nearest Grocery Store: ○ 0-5 mi ○ 5-10 mi ○ 10-20mi ○ 20-30mi ○ 30+ mi

Other grocery or provisions notes: _____

Nearby places visited: _____

_____

_____

Visit/do next time: _____

_____

_____

Connectivity Notes: Wi-Fi: ○Y ○N Rating: 1 2 3 4 5 (1= horrible, 5= excellent)

Cellular signal: Verizon ⬚⬚⬚ AT&T ⬚⬚⬚ Sprint ⬚⬚⬚ T-Mobile ⬚⬚⬚ _____ ⬚⬚⬚

Other Notes: _____

_____

Other notes: _____

_____

_____

_____

_____

_____

_____

_____

_____

_____

_____

_____

Don't forget to add this Log Number to your reference section in the back!

Campground: _____ **Date(s):** ___ / ___ / ___

Location/Address/GPS: _____

Travel to Campground Miles: _____ Time: _____ Travel notes: _____

Cost(s): _____

General Campground/Park Notes:

Hookups: FHU: ○Some ○All ○W/E Only ○50&30 Amp ○30 Amp Only ○Dry Camping
○Dump Station Other hookups notes:_____

Bathhouse: ○Flush Toilets ○Showers (○FREE ○Quarters) Enough Hot Water? ○Y ○N
　　　　Cleanliness: 1 2 3 4 5 (1= very dirty, 5= squeaky clean)
　　　　Other bathhouse notes: _____

Amenities: ○Pool ○Hot Tub ○Lodge/Game Room ○Adult Ctr ○Laundry ○Restaurant
　　　　○Shuffleboard ○Pickleball ○Mini Golf ○Pet-Friendly ○ Dog Park
　　　　○Hiking ○Canoeing ○Fishing ○Horseback Riding ○Fitness Center

Other amenity notes:_____
_____

Management/Booking/Cancellation Notes: _____
_____

Any Campground Scenery? _____
_____

Maneuvering/Parking: ○Tight roads/turns ○Low-hanging trees ○Bad road conditions
Other parking notes:_____
_____
_____

Site-specific Notes:　　　　**Site Number Stayed In:** [＿＿＿＿]

Site Hookups: ○FHU ○W/E Only ○50 Amp ○30 Amp ○Dry Camping

RV Pad: ○Level ○Unlevel ○Concrete ○Rock ○Grass ○Dirt ○Other: _____

Site size: ○Tight ○Moderate ○Spacious ○Very large

Trees/Shade: ○Full Sun ○Some shade ○A lot of shade

Fire ring/pit? ○Y ○N Fires allowed? ○Y ○N Picnic table? ○Y ○N Nice view? ○Y ○N

Close to Amenities? ○Very Close ○Easy Walk ○Too far to walk

Noise: ○Quiet ○Light Road Noise ○Loud Road Noise ○Train ○Other:_____

Any wildlife, bugs, etc? _____

Other site-specific notes: _____

Local Area Notes:

Weather During Stay: ○Very Cold ○Cold ○Moderate ○Warm ○Hot

Other weather notes: _____

Nearby Sightseeing: _____

_____

Nearby Restaurants: _____

_____

Nearest Grocery Store: ○ 0-5 mi ○ 5-10 mi ○ 10-20mi ○ 20-30mi ○ 30+ mi

Other grocery or provisions notes: _____

Nearby places visited: _____

_____

_____

Visit/do next time: _____

_____

_____

Connectivity Notes: Wi-Fi: ○Y ○N Rating: 1 2 3 4 5 (1= horrible, 5= excellent)

Cellular signal: Verizon ▢▢▢ AT&T ▢▢▢ Sprint ▢▢▢ T-Mobile ▢▢▢ _____ ▢▢▢

Other Notes: _____

_____

Other notes: _____

_____

_____

_____

_____

_____

_____

_____

_____

_____

_____

Campground: _____ **Date(s):**   /   /

Location/Address/GPS: _____

Travel to Campground Miles: _____ Time: _____ Travel notes: _____
Cost(s): _____

General Campground/Park Notes:

Hookups: FHU: ○Some ○All ○W/E Only   ○50&30 Amp ○30 Amp Only ○Dry Camping
          ○Dump Station   Other hookups notes:_____

Bathhouse: ○Flush Toilets ○Showers (○FREE ○Quarters) Enough Hot Water? ○Y ○N
            Cleanliness: 1 2 3 4 5 (1= very dirty, 5= squeaky clean)
            Other bathhouse notes: _____

Amenities: ○Pool ○Hot Tub ○Lodge/Game Room ○Adult Ctr ○Laundry ○Restaurant
           ○Shuffleboard ○Pickleball ○Mini Golf ○Pet-Friendly ○Dog Park
           ○Hiking ○Canoeing ○Fishing ○Horseback Riding ○Fitness Center

Other amenity notes:_____
_____

Management/Booking/Cancellation Notes: _____
_____

Any Campground Scenery?_____
_____

Maneuvering/Parking: ○Tight roads/turns ○Low-hanging trees ○Bad road conditions
Other parking notes:_____
_____
_____

Site-specific Notes: Site Number Stayed In: [   ]

Site Hookups: ○FHU   ○W/E Only   ○50 Amp   ○30 Amp   ○Dry Camping
RV Pad: ○Level ○Unlevel   ○Concrete ○Rock ○Grass ○Dirt ○Other: _____
Site size: ○Tight ○Moderate ○Spacious ○Very large
Trees/Shade: ○Full Sun ○Some shade ○A lot of shade
Fire ring/pit? ○Y ○N   Fires allowed? ○Y ○N   Picnic table? ○Y ○N   Nice view? ○Y ○N
Close to Amenities? ○Very Close ○Easy Walk ○Too far to walk
Noise: ○Quiet ○Light Road Noise ○Loud Road Noise ○Train ○Other:_____
Any wildlife, bugs, etc? _____
Other site-specific notes:_____

Local Area Notes:

Weather During Stay: ⭕Very Cold ⭕Cold ⭕Moderate ⭕Warm ⭕Hot

Other weather notes: _____

Nearby Sightseeing: _____

_____

Nearby Restaurants: _____

_____

Nearest Grocery Store: ⭕0-5 mi ⭕5-10 mi ⭕10-20mi ⭕20-30mi ⭕30+ mi

Other grocery or provisions notes: _____

Nearby places visited: _____

_____

_____

_____

Visit/do next time: _____

_____

_____

Connectivity Notes: Wi-Fi: ⭕Y ⭕N Rating: 1 2 3 4 5 (1= horrible, 5= excellent)

Cellular signal: Verizon ▫️▫️▫️ AT&T ▫️▫️▫️ Sprint ▫️▫️▫️ T-Mobile ▫️▫️▫️ _____ ▫️▫️▫️

Other Notes: _____

_____

Other notes: _____

_____

_____

_____

_____

_____

_____

_____

_____

_____

Don't forget to add this Log Number to your reference section in the back!

Campground: _____ **Date(s):** ___ / ___ / ___

Location/Address/GPS: _____

Travel to Campground Miles: _____ Time: _____ Travel notes: _____

Cost(s): _____

General Campground/Park Notes:

Hookups: FHU: ○Some ○All ○W/E Only ○50&30 Amp ○30 Amp Only ○Dry Camping
○Dump Station Other hookups notes:_____

Bathhouse: ○ Flush Toilets ○Showers (○FREE ○Quarters) Enough Hot Water? ○Y ○N
Cleanliness: 1 2 3 4 5 (1= very dirty, 5= squeaky clean)
Other bathhouse notes: _____

Amenities: ○Pool ○Hot Tub ○Lodge/Game Room ○Adult Ctr ○Laundry ○Restaurant
○Shuffleboard ○Pickleball ○Mini Golf ○Pet-Friendly ○ Dog Park
○Hiking ○Canoeing ○Fishing ○Horseback Riding ○Fitness Center

Other amenity notes:_____
_____

Management/Booking/Cancellation Notes: _____
_____

Any Campground Scenery?_____
_____

Maneuvering/Parking: ○Tight roads/turns ○Low-hanging trees ○Bad road conditions
Other parking notes:_____
_____
_____

Site-specific Notes: Site Number Stayed In: [   ]

Site Hookups: ○FHU ○W/E Only ○50 Amp ○30 Amp ○Dry Camping

RV Pad: ○Level○Unlevel ○Concrete ○Rock ○Grass ○Dirt ○Other: _____

Site size: ○Tight ○Moderate ○Spacious ○Very large

Trees/Shade: ○Full Sun ○Some shade ○A lot of shade

Fire ring/pit? ○Y○N Fires allowed?○Y○N Picnic table?○Y○N Nice view? ○Y ○N

Close to Amenities? ○Very Close ○Easy Walk ○Too far to walk

Noise: ○Quiet ○Light Road Noise ○Loud Road Noise ○Train ○Other:_____

Any wildlife, bugs, etc? _____

Other site-specific notes: _____

Local Area Notes:

Weather During Stay: ○Very Cold ○Cold ○Moderate ○Warm ○Hot

Other weather notes:_____

Nearby Sightseeing:_____

_____

Nearby Restaurants:_____

_____

Nearest Grocery Store: ○0-5 mi ○5-10 mi ○10-20mi ○20-30mi ○30+ mi

Other grocery or provisions notes:_____

Nearby places visited:_____

_____

_____

Visit/do next time:_____

_____

_____

Connectivity Notes: Wi-Fi: ○Y ○N   Rating: 1 2 3 4 5 (1= horrible, 5= excellent)

Cellular signal: Verizon ▫▫▫ AT&T ▫▫▫ Sprint ▫▫▫ T-Mobile ▫▫▫ _____ ▫▫▫

Other Notes: _____

_____

Other notes:_____

_____

_____

_____

_____

_____

_____

_____

_____

_____

_____

Don't forget to add this Log Number to your reference section in the back!

Campground: _____ **Date(s):** ___ / ___ / ___

Location/Address/GPS: _____

Travel to Campground Miles: _____ Time: _____ Travel notes: _____

Cost(s): _____

General Campground/Park Notes:

Hookups: FHU: ○Some ○All ○W/E Only ○50&30 Amp ○30 Amp Only ○Dry Camping
○Dump Station Other hookups notes:_____

Bathhouse: ○Flush Toilets ○Showers (○FREE ○Quarters) Enough Hot Water? ○Y ○N

Cleanliness: 1 2 3 4 5 (1= very dirty, 5= squeaky clean)

Other bathhouse notes: _____

Amenities: ○Pool ○Hot Tub ○Lodge/Game Room ○Adult Ctr ○Laundry ○Restaurant
○Shuffleboard ○Pickleball ○Mini Golf ○Pet-Friendly ○Dog Park
○Hiking ○Canoeing ○Fishing ○Horseback Riding ○Fitness Center

Other amenity notes:_____

_____

Management/Booking/Cancellation Notes: _____

_____

Any Campground Scenery?_____

_____

Maneuvering/Parking: ○Tight roads/turns ○Low-hanging trees ○Bad road conditions

Other parking notes:_____

_____

_____

Site-specific Notes: Site Number Stayed In: [_____]

Site Hookups: ○FHU ○W/E Only ○50 Amp ○30 Amp ○Dry Camping

RV Pad: ○Level ○Unlevel ○Concrete ○Rock ○Grass ○Dirt ○Other: _____

Site size: ○Tight ○Moderate ○Spacious ○Very large

Trees/Shade: ○Full Sun ○Some shade ○A lot of shade

Fire ring/pit? ○Y ○N Fires allowed? ○Y ○N Picnic table? ○Y ○N Nice view? ○Y ○N

Close to Amenities? ○Very Close ○Easy Walk ○Too far to walk

Noise: ○Quiet ○Light Road Noise ○Loud Road Noise ○Train ○Other:_____

Any wildlife, bugs, etc? _____

Other site-specific notes: _____

Local Area Notes:

Weather During Stay: ○Very Cold ○Cold ○Moderate ○Warm ○Hot

Other weather notes: _____

Nearby Sightseeing: _____

_____

Nearby Restaurants: _____

_____

Nearest Grocery Store: ○0-5 mi ○5-10 mi ○10-20mi ○20-30mi ○30+ mi

Other grocery or provisions notes:_____

Nearby places visited:_____

_____

_____

Visit/do next time:_____

_____

_____

Connectivity Notes: Wi-Fi: ○Y ○N Rating: 1 2 3 4 5 (1= horrible, 5= excellent)

Cellular signal: Verizon ⸖⸗ AT&T ⸖⸗ Sprint ⸖⸗ T-Mobile ⸖⸗ _____ ⸖⸗

Other Notes: _____

_____

Other notes:_____

_____

_____

_____

_____

_____

_____

_____

_____

_____

_____

Campground: _____ **Date(s):** ___ / ___ / ___

Location/Address/GPS: _____

Travel to Campground Miles: _____ Time: _____ Travel notes: _____

Cost(s): _____

General Campground/Park Notes:

Hookups: FHU: ○Some ○All ○W/E Only ○50&30 Amp ○30 Amp Only ○Dry Camping
○Dump Station   Other hookups notes:_____

Bathhouse: ○Flush Toilets ○Showers (○FREE ○Quarters) Enough Hot Water? ○Y ○N
Cleanliness: 1 2 3 4 5 (1= very dirty, 5= squeaky clean)
Other bathhouse notes: _____

Amenities: ○Pool ○Hot Tub ○Lodge/Game Room ○Adult Ctr ○Laundry ○Restaurant
○Shuffleboard ○Pickleball ○Mini Golf ○Pet-Friendly ○Dog Park
○Hiking ○Canoeing ○Fishing ○Horseback Riding ○Fitness Center

Other amenity notes:_____
_____

Management/Booking/Cancellation Notes: _____
_____

Any Campground Scenery?_____
_____

Maneuvering/Parking: ○Tight roads/turns ○Low-hanging trees ○Bad road conditions
Other parking notes:_____
_____
_____

Site-specific Notes: Site Number Stayed In: [_____]

Site Hookups: ○FHU   ○W/E Only   ○50 Amp   ○30 Amp   ○Dry Camping

RV Pad: ○Level○Unlevel   ○Concrete ○Rock ○Grass ○Dirt ○Other: _____

Site size: ○Tight ○Moderate ○Spacious ○Very large

Trees/Shade: ○Full Sun ○Some shade ○A lot of shade

Fire ring/pit? ○Y○N   Fires allowed?○Y○N   Picnic table?○Y○N Nice view? ○Y ○N

Close to Amenities? ○Very Close ○Easy Walk ○Too far to walk

Noise: ○Quiet ○Light Road Noise ○Loud Road Noise ○Train ○Other:_____

Any wildlife, bugs, etc? _____

Other site-specific notes: _____

Local Area Notes:

Weather During Stay: ○Very Cold ○Cold ○Moderate ○Warm ○Hot

Other weather notes: _____

Nearby Sightseeing: _____

_____

Nearby Restaurants: _____

_____

Nearest Grocery Store: ○0-5 mi ○5-10 mi ○10-20mi ○20-30mi ○30+ mi

Other grocery or provisions notes: _____

Nearby places visited: _____

_____

_____

Visit/do next time: _____

_____

_____

Connectivity Notes: Wi-Fi: ○Y ○N Rating: 1 2 3 4 5 (1= horrible, 5= excellent)

Cellular signal: Verizon ▯▯▯ AT&T ▯▯▯ Sprint ▯▯▯ T-Mobile ▯▯▯ _____ ▯▯▯

Other Notes: _____

_____

Other notes: _____

_____

_____

_____

_____

_____

_____

_____

_____

_____

_____

Don't forget to add this Log Number to your reference section in the back!

Campground: _____ **Date(s):**   /   /

Location/Address/GPS: _____

Travel to Campground Miles: _____ Time: _____ Travel notes: _____

Cost(s): _____

General Campground/Park Notes:

Hookups: FHU: ○Some ○All ○W/E Only   ○50&30 Amp ○30 Amp Only ○Dry Camping
          ○Dump Station Other hookups notes:_____

Bathhouse: ○Flush Toilets ○Showers (○FREE ○Quarters) Enough Hot Water? ○Y ○N
           Cleanliness: 1 2 3 4 5 (1= very dirty, 5= squeaky clean)
           Other bathhouse notes: _____

Amenities: ○Pool ○Hot Tub ○Lodge/Game Room ○Adult Ctr ○Laundry ○Restaurant
           ○Shuffleboard ○Pickleball ○Mini Golf ○Pet-Friendly ○ Dog Park
           ○Hiking ○Canoeing ○Fishing ○Horseback Riding ○Fitness Center

Other amenity notes:_____
_____

Management/Booking/Cancellation Notes: _____
_____

Any Campground Scenery? _____
_____

Maneuvering/Parking: ○Tight roads/turns ○Low-hanging trees   ○Bad road conditions
Other parking notes:_____
_____
_____

Site-specific Notes: Site Number Stayed In: [   ]

Site Hookups: ○FHU   ○W/E Only   ○50 Amp   ○30 Amp   ○Dry Camping

RV Pad: ○Level○Unlevel   ○Concrete ○Rock ○Grass ○Dirt ○Other: _____

Site size: ○Tight ○Moderate ○Spacious ○Very large

Trees/Shade: ○Full Sun ○Some shade ○A lot of shade

Fire ring/pit? ○Y○N   Fires allowed?○Y○N   Picnic table?○Y○N   Nice view? ○Y○N

Close to Amenities? ○Very Close ○Easy Walk ○Too far to walk

Noise: ○Quiet ○Light Road Noise ○Loud Road Noise ○Train ○Other:_____

Any wildlife, bugs, etc? _____

Other site-specific notes: _____

Local Area Notes:

Weather During Stay: ○Very Cold ○Cold ○Moderate ○Warm ○Hot

Other weather notes: _____

Nearby Sightseeing: _____

_____

Nearby Restaurants: _____

_____

Nearest Grocery Store: ○0-5 mi ○5-10 mi ○10-20mi ○20-30mi ○30+ mi

Other grocery or provisions notes: _____

Nearby places visited: _____

_____

_____

Visit/do next time: _____

_____

_____

Connectivity Notes: Wi-Fi: ○Y ○N Rating: 1 2 3 4 5 (1= horrible, 5= excellent)

Cellular signal: Verizon ▫▫▫ AT&T ▫▫▫ Sprint ▫▫▫ T-Mobile ▫▫▫ _____ ▫▫▫

Other Notes: _____

_____

Other notes: _____

_____

_____

_____

_____

_____

_____

_____

_____

_____

_____

Maintenance Logs:

Date serviced: /   /   Location/Address of Service:

Vehicle Serviced: ○RV ○Towed Vehicle ○Tow Vehicle

Serviced by: ○DIY ○Service Business:

Mileage: _____   Cost: $ _____

○Oil Change ○Oil Filter ○Fuel Filter ○Tire Rotation ○New Brakes

Other:_____

_____

_____

_____

_____

Date serviced: /   /   Location/Address of Service:

Vehicle Serviced: ○RV ○Towed Vehicle ○Tow Vehicle

Serviced by: ○DIY ○Service Business:

Mileage: _____   Cost: $ _____

○Oil Change ○Oil Filter ○Fuel Filter ○Tire Rotation ○New Brakes

Other:_____

_____

_____

_____

_____

Date serviced: /   /   Location/Address of Service:

Vehicle Serviced: ○RV ○Towed Vehicle ○Tow Vehicle

Serviced by: ○DIY ○Service Business:

Mileage: _____   Cost: $ _____

○Oil Change ○Oil Filter ○Fuel Filter ○Tire Rotation ○New Brakes

Other:_____

_____

_____

_____

_____

Date serviced: / / Location/Address of Service:

Vehicle Serviced: ○RV ○Towed Vehicle ○Tow Vehicle

Serviced by: ○DIY ○Service Business:

Mileage: _____ Cost: $ _____

○Oil Change ○Oil Filter ○Fuel Filter ○Tire Rotation ○New Brakes

Other: _____

_____

_____

_____

Date serviced: / / Location/Address of Service:

Vehicle Serviced: ○RV ○Towed Vehicle ○Tow Vehicle

Serviced by: ○DIY ○Service Business:

Mileage: _____ Cost: $ _____

○Oil Change ○Oil Filter ○Fuel Filter ○Tire Rotation ○New Brakes

Other: _____

_____

_____

_____

Date serviced: / / Location/Address of Service:

Vehicle Serviced: ○RV ○Towed Vehicle ○Tow Vehicle

Serviced by: ○DIY ○Service Business:

Mileage: _____ Cost: $ _____

○Oil Change ○Oil Filter ○Fuel Filter ○Tire Rotation ○New Brakes

Other: _____

_____

_____

_____

Maintenance Logs:

Date serviced: /   /   Location/Address of Service:
Vehicle Serviced: ○RV ○Towed Vehicle ○Tow Vehicle
Serviced by: ○DIY ○Service Business:
Mileage: _____   Cost: $ _____
○Oil Change ○Oil Filter ○Fuel Filter   ○Tire Rotation   ○New Brakes
Other:_____

_____
_____
_____

Date serviced: /   /   Location/Address of Service:
Vehicle Serviced: ○RV ○Towed Vehicle ○Tow Vehicle
Serviced by: ○DIY ○Service Business:
Mileage: _____   Cost: $ _____
○Oil Change ○Oil Filter ○Fuel Filter   ○Tire Rotation   ○New Brakes
Other:_____

_____
_____
_____

Date serviced: /   /   Location/Address of Service:
Vehicle Serviced: ○RV ○Towed Vehicle ○Tow Vehicle
Serviced by: ○DIY ○Service Business:
Mileage: _____   Cost: $ _____
○Oil Change ○Oil Filter ○Fuel Filter   ○Tire Rotation   ○New Brakes
Other:_____

_____
_____
_____

Date serviced: /   /   Location/Address of Service:

Vehicle Serviced: ◯ RV   ◯ Towed Vehicle   ◯ Tow Vehicle

Serviced by: ◯ DIY   ◯ Service Business:

Mileage: _____   Cost: $ _____

◯ Oil Change   ◯ Oil Filter   ◯ Fuel Filter   ◯ Tire Rotation   ◯ New Brakes

Other: _____

_____

_____

_____

_____

Date serviced: /   /   Location/Address of Service:

Vehicle Serviced: ◯ RV   ◯ Towed Vehicle   ◯ Tow Vehicle

Serviced by: ◯ DIY   ◯ Service Business:

Mileage: _____   Cost: $ _____

◯ Oil Change   ◯ Oil Filter   ◯ Fuel Filter   ◯ Tire Rotation   ◯ New Brakes

Other: _____

_____

_____

_____

_____

Date serviced: /   /   Location/Address of Service:

Vehicle Serviced: ◯ RV   ◯ Towed Vehicle   ◯ Tow Vehicle

Serviced by: ◯ DIY   ◯ Service Business:

Mileage: _____   Cost: $ _____

◯ Oil Change   ◯ Oil Filter   ◯ Fuel Filter   ◯ Tire Rotation   ◯ New Brakes

Other: _____

_____

_____

_____

_____

Maintenance Logs:

Date serviced: /   /   Location/Address of Service:

Vehicle Serviced: ◯RV ◯Towed Vehicle ◯Tow Vehicle

Serviced by: ◯DIY ◯Service Business:

Mileage: _____   Cost: $ _____

◯Oil Change ◯Oil Filter ◯Fuel Filter ◯Tire Rotation ◯New Brakes

Other:_____

_____

_____

_____

Date serviced: /   /   Location/Address of Service:

Vehicle Serviced: ◯RV ◯Towed Vehicle ◯Tow Vehicle

Serviced by: ◯DIY ◯Service Business:

Mileage: _____   Cost: $ _____

◯Oil Change ◯Oil Filter ◯Fuel Filter ◯Tire Rotation ◯New Brakes

Other:_____

_____

_____

_____

Date serviced: /   /   Location/Address of Service:

Vehicle Serviced: ◯RV ◯Towed Vehicle ◯Tow Vehicle

Serviced by: ◯DIY ◯Service Business:

Mileage: _____   Cost: $ _____

◯Oil Change ◯Oil Filter ◯Fuel Filter ◯Tire Rotation ◯New Brakes

Other:_____

_____

_____

_____

Date serviced: / / Location/Address of Service:

Vehicle Serviced: ◯ RV ◯ Towed Vehicle ◯ Tow Vehicle

Serviced by: ◯ DIY ◯ Service Business:

Mileage: _____ Cost: $ _____

◯ Oil Change ◯ Oil Filter ◯ Fuel Filter ◯ Tire Rotation ◯ New Brakes

Other: _____

_____

_____

_____

Date serviced: / / Location/Address of Service:

Vehicle Serviced: ◯ RV ◯ Towed Vehicle ◯ Tow Vehicle

Serviced by: ◯ DIY ◯ Service Business:

Mileage: _____ Cost: $ _____

◯ Oil Change ◯ Oil Filter ◯ Fuel Filter ◯ Tire Rotation ◯ New Brakes

Other: _____

_____

_____

_____

Date serviced: / / Location/Address of Service:

Vehicle Serviced: ◯ RV ◯ Towed Vehicle ◯ Tow Vehicle

Serviced by: ◯ DIY ◯ Service Business:

Mileage: _____ Cost: $ _____

◯ Oil Change ◯ Oil Filter ◯ Fuel Filter ◯ Tire Rotation ◯ New Brakes

Other: _____

_____

_____

_____

Reference Index Log by State

Alabama:

Alaska (General):

Arctic:

Interior:

Western:

Southwestern:

Southcentral:

Southeast:

Arizona:

Arkansas:

California (Southern):

California (Central):

California (Bay Area):

California (Northern):

Colorado:

Connecticut:

Delaware:

Florida (Panhandle):

Florida (Northeast):

Florida (Central):

Florida (South):

Georgia:

Hawaii:

Idaho:

Reference Index Log by State

Illinois: _____
_____
_____

Indiana: _____
_____
_____

Iowa: _____
_____
_____

Kansas: _____
_____
_____

Kentucky: _____
_____
_____

Louisiana: _____
_____
_____

Maine: _____
_____
_____

Maryland: _____
_____
_____

Massachusetts: _____
_____
_____

Michigan: _____
_____
_____

Minnesota:

_____

_____

_____

Mississippi:

_____

_____

Missouri:

_____

_____

Montana:

_____

_____

_____

Nebraska:

_____

_____

Nevada:

_____

_____

New Hampshire:

_____

_____

New Jersey:

_____

_____

New Mexico:

_____

_____

_____

_____

_____

Reference Index Log by State

New York:
_____
_____

North Carolina:
_____
_____
_____

North Dakota:
_____
_____

Ohio:
_____
_____

Oklahoma:
_____
_____

Oregon:
_____
_____
_____

Pennsylvania:
_____
_____

Rhode Island:
_____
_____

South Carolina:
_____
_____
_____

South Dakota:

Tennessee:

Texas (North):

Texas (West):

Texas (Central):

Texas (Gulf Coast):

Texas (Panhandle):

Utah:

Vermont:

Virginia:

Washington:

Reference Index Log by State

West Virginia: _____
_____
_____

Wisconsin: _____
_____
_____

Wyoming: _____
_____
_____

Canada Reference Index Logs

Alberta: _____
_____
_____

British Columbia: _____
_____
_____

Manitoba: _____
_____
_____

New Brunswick: _____
_____
_____

Canada Reference Index Logs

Newfoundland and Labrador:

Nova Scotia:

Ontario:

Prince Edward Island:

Quebec:

Saskatchewan:

Northwest Territories, Nunavut, & Yukon

Reference Index Log for Other Locations (Fill in your own)

Reference Index Log for Other Locations (Fill in your own)

Check out our other editions and cover options as well as our Ultimate Hiking Logbook and Ultimate Campfire Guest Book!

Just search Amazon for your favorite edition's ISBN to order a different design.

Classic Original Cover
ISBN: 978-1790403660

Fulltime Families Edition
Exclusive Family Content!
ISBN:978-1792891847

Leather-look Cover
ISBN: 978-1790808342

Vintage Travel Poster Edition
ISBN: 9798679660632

Ultimate Hiking Logbook
ISBN: 978-1702409865

Campfire Guest Book
ISBN: 979-8656183178

Nomadic Souls
— GEAR & APPAREL —
WWW.NOMADICSOULSGEAR.COM

Made in the USA
Monee, IL
19 October 2020